Big Data and IT Professionals

A Study of the Perceptions Held by IT Professionals in Relation to the Maturity, Value, and Practical Deployment of Big Data Solutions

Damon A. Runion, Ph.D.

ISBN 978-1514870624

Acknowledgments

First, I would like to thank my parents Richard Runion and Shirley Bottenfield. The two of you provided a loving environment for my childhood and offered me countless opportunities to explore my curiosity and grow through learning and doing. It is without a doubt that your love and encouragement has made this achievement possible.

Next, I would like to thank my brothers, Richard, Kevin, Philip, and John. You guys were great role models, friends, and a listening ear when needed. I feel fortunate to be able to call each one of you brother.

Finally, I would like to thank my wife Aki and my children, Takumi and Rika. The three of you are the most important people in my life. I thank you for your sacrifices while I worked on this research project. I am proud to be in your lives.

Table of Contents

1

Introduction

Introduction to the Problem

The explosion of data being captured and stored in information systems has created a new area of challenges and opportunities for information technology (IT) professionals. Every day millions upon millions of bytes of data are being collected, as related to customer transactions, social media postings, government operations, and traffic sensors. The advent of this rise in data is termed "big data" and it presents challenges from technical, managerial, and analytical perspectives. Organizations are being faced with difficult decisions related to the retention of data and how to analyze stored data to extract value. If organizations hope to obtain value from big data, they must understand the breadth and depth of big data awareness held by their IT employees.

Statement of the Problem

There has been little research conducted related to IT professionals and big data. Specifically there have been no studies to determine if relationships exist between IT professionals and their awareness of the maturity, value, hype, future trends, and practical understanding of big data solutions. When IT executives or other leaders in an organization clearly understand the knowledge, skills, and awareness of their staff in relation specific technologies they can develop plans to proceed with the deployment of big data solutions. They can also conduct training and awareness sessions to confirm that their staff has the level of understanding needed to ensure strategic goals are being met as aligned with big data.

Purpose of the Study

This study was designed to evaluate perceptions held by IT professionals in regards to big data. The study focuses on an assessment of IT professionals and their self-assigned understanding of big data in relation to their perceptions of the maturity, value, hype, and future trends of big data. The study also looks at levels of big data understanding in conjunction with occupying a managerial role. The study should prove helpful in determining linkages between training and awareness of big data and the ability of an organization to advance big data initiatives.

Hypotheses

A survey tool will be used to address five hypotheses aimed at answering the intended areas of focus related to big data and the beliefs or perceptions held by IT professionals. The hypotheses are as follows:

Hypothesis H1: An IT professional's understanding of the principles of big data and related technologies is independent of his / her responsibilities in a managerial capacity.

Hypothesis H2: An IT professional's perception of the value of big data solutions is independent of his / her understanding of big data solutions.

Hypothesis H3: An IT professional's expectation of beneficial future development in the area of big data technologies is independent of his / her understanding of big data solutions.

Hypothesis H4: An IT professional's perception of hype in regards to the market recognition of big data technologies is independent of his / her understanding of big data solutions.

Hypothesis H5: An IT professional's perception of the maturity of big data and related technologies is independent of his / her understanding of big data solutions.

Significance of the Study

This study will represent a new contribution to the field of IT management.   It will illustrate levels of significance of critical concepts as they relate to the big data understanding of IT professionals and their perception of the innovation and value of big data solutions.   The study will also help determine reasons why certain organizations have been more successful with big data projects, and move more rapidly along the path of the adoption of advanced analytic solutions.   This study will also provide a baseline at a particular point in time for the pulse of IT professionals. The study is being conducted when there are a lot of advancements and innovation in the tools and techniques used in relation to big data.

Assumptions and Limitations

The survey is focused specifically on IT professionals who self-identified themselves as filing such a role.   The survey also asks respondents to state whether or not they fill a management role. Individuals are requested to rate their understanding of big data and their agreement with certain statements related to big data technologies. As with any study there could be inflation of results, however with the completely anonymous nature of the survey individuals gain no benefit from providing such answers.   A final limitation of the survey is that respondents will self-select for participation in the study.   A wide distribution of messaging via LinkedIn and Twitter will be used to reach as many IT professionals as possible.

Nature of the Study

The study will be conducted in a quantitative manner by administering a survey to IT professionals.

2

Literature Review

Introduction

The literature review provides a solid foundation for under-standing the complexity of big data and how it occupies a critical place in the information technology ecosystem. The section starts off examining the rise of big data its role in modern information technology. Next the review focuses on the qualities of big data with an examination of what "makes" big data. Then the review focuses on the evolution of big data from prior methods and technologies related to data management and analysis. Next the review defines many of the key technologies and operational methods used in the realm of big data. Then the review focuses on the challenges associated with big data technology and solutions. Attention is also given to several key areas that profoundly impact big data. Next the review focuses on the value of big data in three economic areas. In conclusion, the literature review examines big data as a career field for information technology professionals.

The literature review is structured to frame the environment in which big data exists and is presented in both technological and business-oriented constructs. Such a framework is needed to appreciate the variety and nature of responses obtained from the survey respondents.

The Rise of Big Data

Since 1990, roughly aligned with the advent of the modern Internet, the volume of data all around the world has grown tremendously. On a daily basis, businesses capture trillions of bytes of data about their operations, suppliers, customers, and transactions. In addition, there are millions of sensors in countless locations from phones to cars to appliances capturing immediate, real-time values (Chen, Mao, & Liu, 2014). Big data – effectively the accumulation of this data – has grown exponentially (Cukier, 2010). A report by IDC in 2011 stated that the overall amount of data in the entire world was 1.8 zettabytes {approximately 2 billion terabytes} (Gantz & Reinsel, 2011). To put such a significant volume of data into perspective consider the following entities that are equivalent 1.8 zettabytes:

- The stored results of every person on the planet having 215 million Magnetic resonance imaging (MRI) scans per day (Gantz & Reinsel, 2011).

- Two hundred billion High Definition (HD) movies (approximately 2 hours long) {It would take 47 million years for someone to watch 200 billion movies if they watched movies 24 hours a day, non-stop} (Gantz & Reinsel, 2011).

- The storage capacity of about 57 billion Apple iPads with 32 gigabytes of storage.   Fifty-seven billion iPads in terms of physical space could do the following:

>   - Form a wall that would be 61 feet high and extend from Alaska to Florida

>   - Form the basis of a new Great Wall of China that would be just as long as the original but two times taller

>   - Form a wall around all of South America that would be 20 feet high

>   - Completely cover up to 86% of Mexico City

>   - Form a new Mt. Fuji that would be 25 times taller than the real Mt. Fuji (Gantz & Reinsel, 2011)

From 2006 to 2011, global data volume grew a striking nine times. The expectation is that at a biennial pace data volumes will continue increase by at least two hundred percent (Gantz & Reinsel, 2011).

There is no segment of the economy, organization, or any user of technology that has not been impacted by the wave of increased digital information. Consumers of products and services stand to reap benefits from the application of big data (Chen, Mao, & Liu, 2014). There are over 30 million networked sensors operational in the retail, transportation, utility, and other sectors. The growth of these networked sensors is proceeding at an astounding 30 percent rate annually (Chui, Löffler, & Roberts, 2010).

Martin Hilbert and Priscila López studied storage and computing capabilities on a global scale from 1986 to 2007 (Hilbert & López, 2011). Their work showed a significant growth of 23 percent per year over that timeframe, but more interestingly, they found computing capability grew at a faster rate (58% per annum). Their study also examined the effects of increased digitization or the shift from using analog methods of recording data. Calculations based on study data revealed that digital data grew from constituting 25 percent of formatted data in 2000 to an astonishing 94 percent share in 2007.

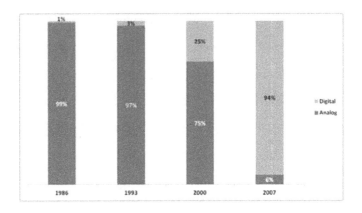

Figure 1: Comparison of Percentage of Analog and Digital Data from 1986 to 2007 (adapted from Hilbert & López, 2011)

This massive growth of data volumes has outstripped previously used technologies such as very large database systems (VLDBs) and brought about the utilization of a new term - big data. Big data is not only an extension of traditional database storage in size but also in structure. Most of what is referred to as big data is unstructured data with a potential greater value if analyzed in real time. Such large data sets offer new approaches to answering questions and gaining significant insight that can only come from the comparison and contrast between many occurrences of an event. With new opportunities related to big data, new risks also emerge particularly in relation to the management of the data (Chen, Mao, & Liu, 2014).

Businesses, industry, and government have all begun to appreciate the benefits of exploiting big data. In addition, many public entities have released details of their plans to cultivate big data and develop relevant applications (Chen, Chiang, & Storey, 2012). Big data has become a frequent topic for research and news media coverage. Popular journals like Nature have published extensive special editions on the subject (Nature, 2008). Such widely dispersed public recognition of big data clearly signifies that we are in the "Age of Big Data" (Chen, Mao, & Liu, 2014).

It makes sense that one the largest sectors of data growth fueling the big data age is the Internet sector. Facebook, the popular social media site, records over ten petabytes of new data every month (Chen, M., Mao, S., & Liu, Y., 2014; Cukier, 2010). Google receives and responds to over 20 petabytes of requests per day (Chen, M., Mao, S., & Liu, Y., 2014; Dean & Ghemawat, 2008). The volume of data has indeed exploded on a global scale. With this drastic, and at times frantic, explosion of data volumes a few critical issues have emerged:

Recent technological innovations such as the Internet of Things (IoT) and cloud computing have also contributed significantly to the growth of the data. IoT refers to the widespread use of sensors in many devices and environments capturing details of activity at particular points in time. IoT is also crossing over to the domain of household use with the prospect of having household appliances, such as refrigerators becoming self-monitoring, alerting consumers to spoilage or low levels of food items. Cloud computing environments are the ideal place to store the feeds from IoT but with the expected data volumes, information systems used to store that data will quickly be outstripped. Little consideration has been made of the ability to extract value from these new sets of data (Chen, M., Mao, S., & Liu, Y., 2014; Chui, Löffler, & Roberts, 2010).

Facebook postings occur globally around the clock due to the ease of use of mobile devices. More powerful mobile devices also make it easier create and upload video content (Mayer-Schönberger & Cukier, 2013). Quickly appearing data presents one of the main challenges related to big data; what is the best way to collect and manage such widely distributed sets of data (Chen, Mao, & Liu, 2014)?

Qualities of Big Data

Big data is a simple term yet the simplicity of the words that comprise the term does not reflect the complexity and depth of its meaning. On its face, big data implies large or burgeoning data sets. While the data sets are big, there are other aspects that define the meaning of big data. At its most basic level, big data refers to sets of data which cannot be managed, accessed, or processed within the "typical" time and resource constraints of traditional software and systems used in the IT industry (Chen,

M., Mao, S., & Liu, Y., 2014; Manyika, et al., 2011). This means the data is either too big or not compliant with storage in a relational database management system (RDBMS).

Big data also has different meanings in various contexts. Exploratory scientists look at large volumes of data differently than data analysts or even systems engineers. Data can be the key to a medical breakthrough or provide insight to potential defects in a manufacturing process. To establish a baseline perspective of big data, it will help to look at the technological aspects and factors related to big data (Chen, Mao, & Liu, 2014).

From a technical perspective, a few key conceptual points underscore big data. Big data is recognized by what are known as the three "V's" – Volume, Variety, and Velocity. Volume relates to the size of the data sets. Variety refers to the mixture of types of data elements, structures, and file types such as spreadsheets, free-text, PDFs, video files, etc. Velocity refers to the both the speed at which new data is being generated and the speed at which it can be consumed to satisfy analytical needs. Because of the three "V's", big data does not fit within established RDBMS frameworks. Structured Query Language (SQL) is used to execute database transactions and requires a standardized method of storage and arrangement of data in order to function properly (Chen, Mao, & Liu, 2014). There are also physical boundaries to database processing, and when thresholds of data exceed a defined level, query performance begins to degrade as the database kernel either exceeds memory space or processor boundaries (McLellan, 2013). An agreed upon range of data volume that corresponds to big data is data that is between the hundreds of terabytes to several petabytes in size (Manyika, et al., 2011). The research firm Gartner, a trusted independent advisor on technology, offered a clear definition of big data: " 'Big data' is high - volume, -velocity and -variety information assets that demand cost-effective, innovative forms of information processing for enhanced insight and decision-making" (Gartner, 2013).

However, some do not entirely agree with this definition of big data. IDC defined big data as "a new generation of technologies and architectures, designed to economically extract value from very large volumes of a wide variety of data, by enabling high-velocity capture, discovery, and/or analysis" (Gantz & Reinsel, 2011). IDC's definition goes beyond the Gartner definition by including recognition of the value of data. This recognition highlights the fact that capturing data for the sake of capturing it makes very little sense in most circumstances. Big data must be utilized to unearth hidden patterns or relationships within data sets that are created rapidly, contain varying types of content, and are massive in scale. As explained by Jay Parikh, Vice President of Infrastructure Engineering at Facebook, "If you aren't taking advantage of the data you're collecting, then you just have a pile of data, you don't have big data" (Chen, M., Mao, S., & Liu,

Y., 2014; Constine, 2012).

The US National Institute of Standards and Technology (NIST) provides the following definition of big data: "Big data is the term used to describe the deluge of data in our networked, digitized, sensor-laden, information driven world. The availability of vast data resources carries the potential to answer questions previously out of reach" (National Institute of Standards and Technology, 2014).

This definition places more emphasis on the technology components of big data rather than business or operational value. As envisioned by NIST, big data will only be able to provide meaningful value if new technologies or methods can be created to capture, manage, and process these large data sets (Chen, Mao, & Liu, 2014).

Development of Big Data

The general idea of big data has its roots in the "database machine" movement of the early 1980's (Su, et al., 1980). The database machine was to be a purpose built hardware and software technology unit designed to store and allow analysis of data. The database machine was conceptualized because the limitations of individual mainframe computers became evident to many system administrators (Goda, 2009). Mainframes are based on the concept of time-sharing or shared resources, with data volumes rising many organizations soon realized that a small pool of users was quickly using more than their share of system resources.   This realization led to the concept of a "share nothing" or a standalone parallel database framework (DeWitt & Gray, 1992).   A share nothing architecture provides each database environment with dedicated storage, memory, and processing capabilities.   Oracle and Teradata emerged as the commercial leaders in the share nothing database space (Chen, Mao, & Liu, 2014).

Despite the increased size and processing capabilities offered by novel approaches to database management, new issues quickly appeared.   The advent of the World Wide Web and the associated query indexing and caching of results led to a rapid growth of databases dedicated to storing data related to those tasks. Google created the Google File System (GFS) and MapReduce software components to address the content storage and access issues related to query technology (Dean & Ghemawat, 2008). Aside from the growth of data as a result of Internet searches, there was also tremendous growth arising from other areas. There was a rise in user generated content, storage of information from networking and telecommunication devices, and widespread transactional data causing traditional data management technologies and frameworks to burst at the seams.   In 2011 EMC in conjunction with IDC released a detailed study entitled Extracting Values from Chaos (Gantz & Reinsel, 2011).   This study was the first written document that utilized the term "big data." Both business and higher education recognized the new concept of big data and realized the profound impact it would have on computing and also society (Chen, Mao, & Liu, 2014).

By early to mid-2010, virtually all leading software and Internet companies commenced significant efforts to create powerful big data offerings. Most notably Oracle created the Big Data Appliance, a hardware/software engineered system running an Open Source version of Hadoop (Garlasu, et al., 2013). Microsoft, Amazon, EMC, and Google have also spearheaded both internal and commercial offerings to claim a stake in the big data marketplace. In addition, a large number of startup firms sprang up to develop solutions in the big data space. Academic researchers have focused on machine learning and artificial intelligence which highlight much of the big data value proposition (Bryant, Katz, & Lazowska, 2008; Chen, M., Mao, S., & Liu, Y., 2014).

Big data also garnered the focus of many governments all around the world. The United States commenced a focused effort by setting aside US$200 million to seek innovative and highly useful big data solutions. In early 2012, President Obama's technical advisors announced the "Big Data Research and Development Initiative" (Lazar, 2012). Later in 2012, the United Nations published a report outlining the ways in which big data can be utilized to provide greater benefits for citizens (Chen, M., Mao, S., & Liu, Y.,

2014; United Nations, 2013).

Technologies Used With Big Data

Big data processing, storage, analysis, and retention rely on a widely dispersed group of technologies and methods which span several disciplines, including computer science, statistics, mathematics, and management. Any organization with intentions to derive value from big data must recognize the fact that an interdisciplinary approach will likely yield optimal results. Much of the processes and frameworks developed for traditional data management with appropriate updates and modifications can be applied to large data. However, new categories and techniques for data management and analysis have been created from principles of advanced computer engineering, mathematics, and statistics. Academic institutions have also spearheaded efforts to create computing paradigms to meet the needs of business and governments.

The realm of technologies related to big data is constantly evolving from both a physical hardware perspective as well as a software perspective. The following section will attempt to detail much of the notable technologies and practices in the realm of big data.

Software and Systems Used to Support Big Data

Big data is a constantly evolving field. There are frequent enhancements to existing technology and creation of new methods and tools to assist in the management, storage, and analysis of large data sets. The following list of technologies is not comprehensive nor is it exclusively dedicated to big data (Manyika, et al., 2011).

Relational database: A relational database is data storage mechanism that orients data storage into a series of tables. A collection of tables is organized into a schema and tables have defined relationships through key columns. Every table contains a data field called a primary key that uniquely identifies the rows in the table. These primary keys also serve as foreign keys in other tables where there is a logical relationship between the two tables. Tables can also have indexes defined as part of their structure. Indexes are used by the query engine to quickly locate records to satisfy a request. Relational database engines along with their disk storage and memory management components comprise a relational database management system (RDBMS). RDBMSs are accessed primarily through Structured Query Language (SQL) or vendor proprietary extensions to SQL such as PL/SQL (Procedural Language/SQL) for use in an Oracle database environment (Manyika, et al., 2011).

Structured Query Language (SQL): SQL is a standalone programming language created for the storage, editing, and deletion of data in RDBMSs.   SQL was developed using principles of relational algebra and tuple relational calculus.   Edgar Codd drafted a conceptual paper, A Relational Model of Data for Large Shared Data Banks in 1970; this work is recognized as the first documentation of what would become SQL.   In 1979, Relational Software, Inc., released a version of SQL named Oracle (to which the company later changed its name).   This was the first version of SQL available to the public (Chamberlin, 2012).   SQL contains three subset frameworks, data definition language (DDL), data manipulation language (DML), and data control language (DCL).   DDL is the set of commands used to create, alter, and delete tables or views.   DML are commands used to alter the column level elements of a table for singular or multi-row operations.   DCL is a set of security commands allowing users the power to grant other users rights to modify tables and other objects (Manyika, et al., 2011).

Business intelligence: Business intelligence (BI) is a group of technologies, architectures, and design methodologies where raw data is transformed or utilized directly to create additional business value through data analysis.   BI is typically used to create reports and dashboards comprised of tabular and graphical displays of data that can be manipulated in an interactive manner with list, checkbox, and other selection mechanisms.   BI is often utilized to support business processes such as human resource management, financial operations, and supply chain and order management. Many firms and organizations use BI to help refine their operations and gain insight into internal and external operations in order to achieve advantages over their competitors (Manyika, et al., 2011).

Non-relational / NoSQL database: A Non-relational or NoSQL ("Not only SQL") database is a data storage framework using a categorization method not based on tables related by common or shared columns as is used in a relational database. Common types of data structures can be document storage (as in the case of JavaScript Object Notation (JSON) documents), graphs, or key-value pairs. The desire to use a NoSQL approach stems from a few factors ranging from higher availability to a faster capability to scale a growing data set with additional hardware (Manyika, et al., 2011).

MapReduce: MapReduce is method of programming used on clustered data sets by distributing an algorithm to subsets of the data for execution or further lower level distribution. MapReduce derives its name from its combined processing model of executing Map and Reduce procedures. A Map procedure executes a filtering routine on a data set or file (such as ordering a list of transactions by products). A Reduce procedure then executes an aggregating mathematical procedure (such as counting the total number of products by each type). While MapReduce is essentially a very simple programming concept, the true value is gained through the parallelization and distributed nature of its operation, thus enabling massive data sets to be processed. The name MapReduce itself was exclusively associated with the Google owned technology for which it was developed; however numerous clones have been developed using alternate programming languages so that the term is now a generic computing process. (Dean & Ghemawat, 2008; Manyika, et al., 2011).

Hadoop: Hadoop is an open-source data storage framework based on a distributed system paradigm. Hadoop is managed by the Apache Software Foundation. Hadoop consists of the following core modules:

- Hadoop Common: libraries and inter-module utilities
- Hadoop Distributed File System (HDFS): the controller for data management across commodity machines
- Hadoop YARN: the resource management component applying compute resources to the managed clusters
- Hadoop MapReduce: the programming interface used to introspect and analyze large data sets (Manyika, et al., 2011)

Cassandra: Cassandra, a data management framework, is based on the NoSQL architecture and utilizes commodity hardware to create large data stores. Cassandra is open source software managed by the Apache Software Foundation. Cassandra uses a row store methodology for storing data where each table is organized by a primary key with an initial value of a partition key. Table contents are clustered based on the key value, but additional indexing options exist for the core columns of the table. The University of Toronto conducted research which shows that Cassandra is the fastest of all NoSQL databases available for use by the public (Hewitt, 2010; Manyika, et al., 2011).

Bigtable: Bigtable is proprietary data storage framework built by Google and designed to run on the Google File System. It is operates as a multi-dimensional sorted map with data elements being stored across hundreds to thousands of machines. This framework can scale into the petabyte range. Data elements in the framework are indexed using a set of three elements, a timestamp, a column key, and a row key. This indexing strategy is very similar to the methods used in relational databases (Chang, et al., 2008; Manyika, et al., 2011).

Cloud computing: Cloud computing is the framework and operations of delivering computing capabilities (software, servers, and programming environments) as a service via an open network, the Internet, or over a private network. The main concept of cloud computing is that computing shall be available via an on-demand, as-needed basis like electrical power. It is through the clustering of servers and shared access to an instance that cloud computing provides greater value over traditional on-premise computing models (Manyika, et al., 2011).

Data warehouse: A data warehouse is a purpose-built data-base used for reporting and analysis. A data warehouse pulls data from transactional systems of record, as well as supporting systems, to allow for a unified view of an organization's business. Occasionally a data warehouse is referred to as an Enterprise Data Warehouse (EDW). Data warehouses are often used to create reports for senior management focusing on the overall health of lines of the business. Data warehouses also excel at linking data together that corresponds to multiple facets of a transaction, such as inventory on hand, shipment delays, product defects, sales effectiveness, and customer satisfaction. Data is loaded into a data warehouse using data movement logic called an Extract, Transform, and Load or ETL routine. Frequently an operational data store (ODS) is put in place before the denormalization of data going into the data warehouse to allow for more transaction-oriented reporting (Manyika, et al., 2011).

Data mart: A data mart is business unit or departmentally focused database used for analysis of transactional or other data via business intelligence tools. Frequently a data mart is a subset of a data warehouse, but occasionally data marts are deployed in a standalone manner with the sponsoring department responsible not only for the data in the system also the hardware and software (Manyika, et al., 2011).

Excel: Excel is a central program in the Microsoft Office Suite. Excel is primarily a spreadsheet application, but has grown over the years through its ease of use to be a primary data analysis tool. According to a 2012 survey of 798 statistics and analytics professionals by KDNuggets (2012), 29% reported using Excel as their primary analysis tool; this made it the number 2 tool of choice. Excel can also be extended using the Microsoft supplied Analysis ToolPak to allow it to perform a range of statistical tests, including Analysis of Variance, Correlation, F-Test, and Regression (Chen, Mao, & Liu, 2014).

Extract, Transform, and Load (ETL): ETL refers to a computing process that is part of database administration responsibilities. ETLs perform the following tasks: 1) Extract data from a system of record or another system where transactions are stored. 2) Transform data to resolve errors or join elements together that are commonly used in conjunction with analysis. 3) Load data into a target database schema such as a data mart, an operational data store, or an Enterprise Data Warehouse (Manyika, et al., 2011).

Metadata: Metadata fundamentally is data about data. While sounding ambiguous, metadata consists of the descriptive elements that categorize a set of data or data elements for another purpose. Metadata exists in two main forms. One is structural metadata. Structural metadata defines the types and format of data such as the database column type or parameters of a field in a table. The other form is descriptive metadata. Descriptive metadata offers categorization or other types of qualities about the actual data content of a cell. An example of descriptive metadata element would be the classification of certain telephone records as being from a specific geographic location (Manyika, et al., 2011).

R: R is an open source programming language used to perform statistical analysis on a wide variety of data sets. R has become the analysis tool of choice for most statisticians and data miners due its simple interpreter framework and low cost of ownership. R supports almost all statistical techniques. According to a 2012 survey of 798 statistics and analytics professionals by KDNuggets (2012), 31% reported using R as their primary analysis tool; this made it the number 1 tool of choice. Given the dominance of R in this space, database vendors like Oracle and Teradata recently added R support to their product offerings (Chen, Mao, & Liu, 2014).

Semi-structured data: Semi-structured data is a form of data that does not readily comply with the requirements of relational databases in terms of size, format, and volatility. Semi-structured data does however have characteristics that allow categorization and placement into hierarchies. It does however have internal metadata qualities that allow for rapid record identification. Two examples of semi-structured data are XML documents and JSON documents (Manyika, et al., 2011).

Structured data: Structured data is a form of data stored in a fixed format. This allows the data elements to be accessed in a declarative manner and allows the creation of indexes or pointers to rapidly find particular data values. Relational databases and spreadsheets represent the two most common forms of structured data (Manyika, et al., 2011).

Unstructured data: Unstructured data is data without a formal structure or assigned index. Unstructured data must be analyzed in its entirety to be categorized. Some examples of unstructured data include email messages, comment fields on forms, or un-tagged video and audio (Manyika, et al., 2011).

Procedures, Tests, and Methods for Big Data Analysis

Most of the procedures, tests, and methods used to perform analytics on big data rely on computer science and statistics. The list below is not exclusively oriented toward big data and many of the entries are proven standard statistical techniques (Manyika, et al., 2011).

Statistics: Statistics is a scientific branch of inquiry related to the collection, organization, analysis, and presentation of data. Statistics is closely related to mathematics although it is regarded to be a separate field in its own right. Statistics is concerned with determining the relationships between factors known as variables and how strongly relationships between variables impact each other. Statistical significance is considered to be the case when one factor drives the outcome of another factor (California State University - Long Beach, n.d.; Manyika, et al., 2011).

A/B Testing: A/B Testing represents a statistical testing procedure where a control group is measured against one or more test groups to evaluate what interactions will affect a variable of interest. A/B Testing has been used quite heavily in e-Commerce and is usually focused on what types of web presentation techniques influence consumer decision. Analysts have looked at layouts, image placement, colors, and fonts as influencing parameters (Manyika, et al., 2011; Martin, Hanington, & Hanington, 2012). In the context of big data, A/B Testing can be used to rapidly test a large set of data by quickly creating groups split along a small set of values. Using other statistical methods, analysts can ensure their decisions are statistically significant and in turn validate a large data set.

Association rule learning: ARL is a statistical testing method where groups are analyzed using a variety of algorithms to create expected outcomes or rules. ARL is considered to be a data mining procedure (Agrawal, Imieliński, & Swami, 1993). One of the most common association rules is market basket analysis, which is a routine typically used by retailers to determine if there is any association between the items customers purchase together. One goal of ARL is to identify patterns to generate promotional efforts based on product affinity (Manyika, et al., 2011). In the context of big data, ARL can help identify clusters or groups within larger populations for segmentation and further analysis.

Classification: Classification is a set of statistical procedures utilizing a small set of data, called a training set, to group large data sets along desired categories. A statistician will create a training set using specific parameters. Then the training set is applied to a larger data set using a rules-driven engine. Classification is most commonly used with data sets related to customer decisions and behavior. Standard tests assess churn rate, buying patterns, frequency of service requests, or rates of product returns. Classification in the context of automation is referred to as a supervised learning process since the operator provides a training set and the process does not examine the data set on its own to identify categories (Alpaydin, 2004; Manyika, et al., 2011).

Cluster analysis: Cluster analysis is used to classify a large and diverse set of elements into smaller similarly organized units. Cluster analysis is similar to classification, but it does not utilize a training set and data elements are repeatedly sorted and examined by processes until natural divisions begin to appear. Cluster analysis is most commonly used for customer segmentation when the volume of customers is quite high (Bailey, 1994; Manyika, et al., 2011).

Crowdsourcing: Crowdsourcing is a method where interested individuals are contacted, typically via social media, to participate in or contribute to a project or research effort. One example of crowdsourcing is an effort by Lego Corporation that allows customers to submit new ideas for toys. Once an idea receives 10,000 votes it moves to an internal corporate review process (Schoultz, 2014). In the context of big data, crowdsourcing can result in vast amounts of rapidly collected data which in turn creates storage and processing demands (Manyika, et al., 2011).

Data fusion: Data fusion is a process where data from multiple sources is combined and analyzed to detect patterns or uncover hidden qualities. One example is the process of taking data from a social media platform such as Twitter and correlating a spike in tweets with a rise in sales of a particular item (Manyika, et al., 2011). Data fusion is an especially well-suited practice with respect to big data because it can help provide value through rapid insight into heterogeneous data.

Data mining: Data mining is a subset of computer science in which large data sets are analyzed for patterns using techniques such as machine learning, statistics, and artificial intelligence. The end state of a data mining process is a reduced set of actionable information in a consumption ready format. A frequently discussed application of data mining is credit card fraud detection. This type of data mining occurs through the deep analysis of spending habits of a customer, including factors such as location and amounts spent (Manyika, et al., 2011).

Ensemble learning: Ensemble learning is the process of joining together several predictive models to further extract data from a complex data set. The individual predictive models are derived from machine learning or statistical models. Ensemble learning is regarded as being a supervised learning activity (Manyika, et al., 2011; Oza & Russell, 2000).

Machine learning: Machine learning, a subset of artificial intelligence, focuses on the creation and analysis of programs and systems that can learn and provide output for decision-making. An example of machine learning would be the process of training a system to determine if email messages are spam messages or genuine email traffic. Once tests have confirmed reliability, a routine can be implemented to automatically process messages and filter messages that are spam into a separate email folder (Alpaydin, 2004; Manyika, et al., 2011).

Natural language processing (NLP): NLP is a subset of artificial intelligence that draws heavily on the field of linguistics. NLP examines the ability of computers to understand and interact with humans in a verbal form. One goal of NLP is to minimize the degree of manual interaction a human must have with a computer, limiting it to a series of spoken commands. Another goal of NLP is to allow computers to converse with humans in a natural manner. Voice prompting in the case of fielding initial calls to a customer service line is an example of NLP (Chowdhury, 2003; Manyika, et al., 2011).

Artificial neural networks: ANNs are software-based models based on the structure and activity processes of living beings. ANNs are developed to mimic the processes of the brain and seek to validate advanced machine learning and recognition of visual phenomena such as pattern recognition. Depending on the complexity of the ANN and the desired tasks, an ANN can represent a supervised or unsupervised learning framework. An example of an application built using an ANN would be a program designed to detect fraud in Medicare claims (Dayhoff & DeLeo, 2001; Manyika, et al., 2011).

Social network analysis: Social network analysis corresponds to the application of electronic network theory to establish a pattern of relationships between two or more participants in social networks. Through social network analysis, individual people are considered to be nodes in a web of relationships connected by ties to the environmental framework. Nodes are evaluated by their thickness to depict values such as counts of relationships or length of time associated with those relationships (Manyika, et al., 2011; Marcus, Moy, & Coffman, 2007).

Predictive modeling: Predictive modeling is where a structured set of rules are applied to a data set to create a model for repeated testing. Predictive modeling strives to determine a particular outcome or evaluate how likely an outcome might appear in future situations. Examples of predictive modeling include random forests, Naive Bayes, and majority classifier (Dickey, 2012; Manyika, et al., 2011).

Regression: Regression is a form of statistical testing used to evaluate the relationships among variables. Typically regression is used to measure the effects that independent variables have on one or more dependent variables. This analysis allows a researcher to reach a level of statistical confidence that an incident is caused by another factor. Regression is frequently used in manufacturing processes to identify input parameters that could be contributing to defects in outputted products (Manyika, et al., 2011).

Sentiment analysis: Sentiment analysis is a data analysis framework where text analysis and natural language processing are used determine subjective or emotional meaning in a data set.

Sentiment analysis is used widely with data sets pulled from social media platforms. In this context, a series of tweets or postings are analyzed to determine the overall feeling regarding a product or statement. For instance, a cell phone vendor may use sentiment analysis to gauge customer reaction to plans it recently announced for a phone with a new advanced video recording feature (Manyika, et al., 2011).

Spatial analysis: Spatial analysis is the application of statistical techniques to data that has been encoded with geographical qualities so that relationships can be measured in space and time. Geographic information systems (GISs) store and manage geographic properties of homes, retail establishments, and/or public places. Spatial analysis utilizes data from a GIS along with other data sets such as product sales and applies techniques like regression to determine the relationships between elements such as purchasing habits and residence location. For instance, individuals who live close to a swimming pool might be more likely to purchase sun block or swimming accessories at the start of the swim season (Manyika, et al., 2011).

Supervised learning: Supervised learning, a machine learning process, is where a program or procedure is taught how to rank or measure a set of data through the use of a training set created by a human. Supervised learning is frequently used for refined classification of items where a number of subjective factors are used to determine the desired groupings (Cortes & Vapnik, 1995; Manyika, et al., 2011).

Simulation: Simulation is a method of modeling the outcome of a series of interrelated events with a wide degree of permutations or options. Simulations are typically conducted a multitude of times with slight modifications made to variables with each run. One commonly used set of simulations are Monte Carlo simulations. Monte Carlo simulations are a set of algorithms using repeated random sampling following differing assumptions to arrive at a consistently occurring phenomenon. The output of simulations is usually provided in a histogram which allows for rapid visual identification of an outlier or leading candidate (Manyika, et al., 2011).

Time series analysis: Time series analysis, a data analysis procedure, is based on analyzing a series of entities over a set period of time in order to detect trends or causes behind certain occurrences. Time series analysis can also be used in a forecasting manner where a repeated series of concurrent events can be used derive a statistical significance of recurrence. Time series analysis is frequently used in sales management environments to measure and predict the flow of a sales cycle. It has also been used in the life sciences arena to predict and determine the progression of both illnesses and treatments (Manyika, et al., 2011).

Unsupervised learning: Unsupervised learning, a type of machine learning, is when an algorithm is used to analyze a data set. The algorithm develops groupings and structure on its own rather than through the use of a training set inputted by a human. One example of unsupervised learning is cluster analysis (Manyika, et al., 2011).

Visualization: Visualization is a key presentation option when dealing with big data. Visualization is the process of using charts, images, diagrams, or other animated displays to convey details about a set or subset of data. Visualizations help overcome human limitations with respect to analyzing large data sets. Visualizations can be used to identify outliers or show the relative intensity of one data group to another (Manyika, et al., 2011). Some commonly used examples of visualizations are as follows:

- Tag cloud: A tag cloud, as shown in the image below, is a list of terms in a data set with the most commonly occurring terms displayed in larger font (Manyika, et al., 2011).

Figure 2: Example of a Tag Cloud

- Scatter plot: A scatter plot is diagram where data is displayed as a grouping of elements aligned with a measure on each
axis. Occasionally color or another indicator will be used to show
intensity thus becoming a third axis. Scatter plots are very useful
with large data sets because they clearly highlight outliers or ex-
tremely different cases (Manyika, et al., 2011).

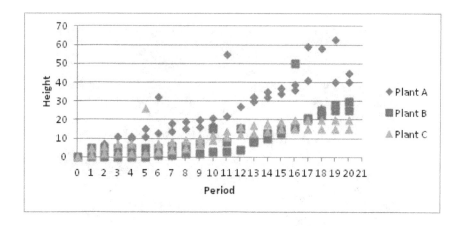

Figure 3: Example of a Scatter plot

Challenges of Big Data

As stated earlier big data is not only characterized by large volumes of data but fast acquisition of that data. The rate and volumes of data pose significant challenges for the information technology industry. The relational database management system (RDBMS) model is still the primary means of storing data. Generally speaking RDBMSs are limited by the size that they can grow and the types of data they can store. RDBMSs for the most part excel at the storage and provision of structured data sets. The RDBMS paradigm runs counter to the nature of much of the newly generated data in the world which is unstructured and difficult to be categorized. RDBMSs also typically require the core processing engine or kernel to be located on a single machine.

This presents challenges in regards to disk size, processing power, and memory – ultimately resulting in an expensive solution. With these challenges in mind, technology researchers have developed solutions such as distributed storage mechanisms via cloud computing or elastic processing frameworks. Database vendors have also worked to create new file systems to store data in native formats and use less rigorous NoSQL frameworks to allow for more rapid access to data (Cattell, 2011; Chen, Mao, & Liu, 2014).

The primary issues related to the development of big data applications, which are applications seeking to derive value from big data assets, can be typically characterized in the following categories.

The first is that data are not well structured, or that structure is not readily apparent. With the wide variety of types of data being captured there are very divergent forms of specificity, organization, and structures to that data. Such wide variety makes the use of that data very challenging especially as it relates to joined or heterogeneous access. Structured data representation is an approach where creating a valid taxonomy of data elements can help derive value from the data. Data representation is critical because the improper classification of data can result in negative benefits being gained from analysis (Chen, Mao, & Liu, 2014; Jagadish, et al., 2014).

The second is that data are often repeated or waste space un- necessarily. Data is often duplicated in most data sets, even in RDBMSs. This issue is vastly compounded in the context of big data. For instance, on Facebook many individuals share and re- share notable news events and effectively duplicate the same core information over and over. Data storage is one of the most costly aspects of big data and the storage of repeating values leads to waste of storage, processing, and network resources (Chen, Mao, & Liu, 2014; Jagadish, et al., 2014).

Third, data do not have "effective" or "usable" conditions. The rapid rate at which data is increasing creates a challenge with re- spect to the freshness or currency of the data. Conditions or pa- rameters must be created to designate the retention period of da- ta and how pertinent it can be for use in analysis. Data freshness can be established by date of acquisition or another scoring framework with an ultimate goal of determining a purge or ar- chive date to reclaim used space (Chen, Mao, & Liu, 2014; Jagadish, et al., 2014).

Fourth are electrical power issues. For decades, computing has been an activity heavily dependent on electrical power. High us- age of electricity is both economic and environmental issue. As data sets grow the amount resources needed to transport, store, and process that data is likely to grow in a similar exponential fashion. The design of new systems and frameworks for handling big data must address this resource consumption issue because there is no limitless source of electrical power (Chen, Mao, & Liu, 2014; Koomey, 2011).

Fifth is future proofing. The development of big data systems must not only address current needs but allow for growth and expansion in the future. Logical as well as physical components must have interfaces and methods to allow for future extension (Chen, Mao, & Liu, 2014).

Sixth is the need for an interdisciplinary approach to handling issues. Big data involves a wide variety of disciplines to be successful, and one individual is not likely to possess the entire set of skills to establish and maintain a big data architecture. From statistical experts to database administrators, a team-oriented approach will serve best in meeting an organization's strategic and tactical goals related to big data. (Chen, Mao, & Liu, 2014).

The last major issue is security. Security is one of the most pressing matters in the area of big data. Unlike RDBMSs where object level security is strictly enforced, big data can often be undertaken in environments with the most minimum of security constraints. Security concerns are a key factor that must be addressed and should be related to datatypes stored in the system. Controls must be robust if financial or health-related information is present in the data sets. In addition, responsible parties must consider the security aspects of an analysis that can be derived from a data set. It is possible that the security issues may not be evident at the outset, but the universe of possibilities must be examined prior to deploying a big data solution (Chen, Mao, & Liu, 2014; Tankard, 2012).

Where Does Big Data Come From?

Big data does not simply appear from nowhere, it must be generated. Every day billions of new records are created in relation to Internet usage. New data also comes from forum posts on social media sites, blogs, search results, and brand new content. Data is the currency of daily life and speaks volumes not only about our actions, but who we are as individuals. On an atomic level, an individual piece of data may or may not have much value but when it is combined with a larger set of values that data can help reveal significant trends. Through the analysis of big data it is possible to predict what products a consumer may be highly inclined to purchase next and offer a targeted offer at the proper moment.

Despite the fact that data is quite varied, there are four main categories of data in the realm of big data. These are enterprise data, health and life science data, IoT data, and advanced scientific research (Chen, Mao, & Liu, 2014).

Enterprise Data

Enterprise data represents the single largest source of all data. In the paper entitled The real-world use of big data, IBM outlined the extent to which in most cases that big data relates to business or governmental processes. Within this grouping, the vast majority of this data pertains to business activities ranging from financial operations, production processes, customer relationship management, and human resource management. Generally most of this data is held in enterprise resource planning systems (ERPs) from large software vendors like Oracle and SAP and stored in an RDBMS (Schroeck, Shockley, Smart, Romero-Morales, & Tufano, 2012). Until recently this data was a significantly underutilized asset in most organizations with little consideration given to analysis beyond that which was possible within a spreadsheet (Chen, Mao, & Liu, 2014).

Over the last 15 years, business intelligence has vaulted to the forefront of technologies to exploit the value of data stored within ERPs or other transactional systems. Based upon research by McKinsey, it was concluded that the amount of data held by the typical corporation will grow by 200 percent over an 18-month period (Manyika, et al., 2011). Gantz and Reinsel concluded that a value of over US$450 billion is attributable to business conducted over the Internet. Enterprise data is inherently part of the extreme growth of data sets worldwide (Gantz & Reinsel, 2011).

For instance, Walmart processes over one million customer transactions per hour. This data is added to what is regarded as one
of the largest data warehouses in the world at 2.5 petabytes
(Cukier, 2010). Another retailer, Amazon, which focuses almost
entirely on Internet based operations, handles over 500,000
transactions every second (Chen, Mao, & Liu, 2014; Rosoff,
2012).

Mckinsey estimated that in 2009 across all sectors of industry
nearly every employer of more than 1,000 people had at least 200
terabytes of data. The study also found an increasing number of
firms with more than 1 petabyte of enterprise data. One interesting finding in the McKinsey study is that approximately 80 percent
of that data appeared to be duplicated, such that it was being
maintained in more than one system across the enterprise. The
McKinsey study also estimated that the global level of enterprise
data exceeded 7 exabytes (Manyika, et al., 2011). Further analysis of these pools of enterprise data revealed a heavier weighting
of data volume in certain business sectors. The financial industry
(including banking, stock trading, and other investments) stored
the most data per employee across the group of industries that
were surveyed. This ranking is likely related to the highly transaction-oriented nature of the financial industry. The New York
Stock Exchange has a publicly stated rate of processing 500 million trades per month on average. Another frontrunner in the
area of data capture and retention are government agencies,

communications/media firms, and utility providers. These groups store a great of benefit, service, and content related data for their customers and constituents. Particularly in the area of media there has been an explosion of on-demand video and audio offerings to widely diverse audiences. Finally, the sector with the highest ranking in terms of overall enterprise data in storage is the manufacturing sector. Data captured in manufacturing environments is related to development, testing, and production processes. Since manufacturing efforts are often automated there tends to be little direct linkage of this data to individual employees (Manyika, et al., 2011).

IoT Data

As briefly introduced earlier, the Internet of Things (IoT) is a new and rapidly growing source of big data. IoT is penetrating all aspects of commerce and industry and is poised to play a significant role in the development of smart transportation systems, public services, utility distribution, agriculture, and consumer markets.

IoT data has markedly different features than enterprise data, and these factors create challenges with respect to storage and particularly the analysis of the data sets.

IoT data is highly heterogeneous. Even within a single organization the types of data stored from IoT inputs can vary widely. As mentioned earlier some, IoT data can be simple records of environmental factors. In the case of smart transportation systems, IoT data can consist of multiple data points gathered from a broad range of automobiles. This data can include details like the speed of an automobile, if automobiles were accelerating or slowing down, the position of one automobile to another, and weather factors. Such variety requires careful consideration of storage as well as how the data can be analyzed (Chen, Mao, & Liu, 2014).

IoT data typically contains a great deal of metadata. As mentioned in the previous paragraph IoT sensors are used to not only capture information about a single physical entity but also the time and space relationships between entities. For instance, a package delivery firm may use IoT sensors to evaluate the positioning of delivery trucks on assigned routes, to improve delivery scheduling, and shorten task completion times. Analysis of such inter-relationships between data elements via advanced statistical measures can reveal trends and points that are otherwise impossible to detect (Chen, Mao, & Liu, 2014).

IoT data frequently contains a great deal of noise. As can be expected with sensors a great deal of data that is captured provides little value. One such case might be a sensor system designed to detect speeding drivers along a highway. Only a handful of exceptional outliers will flagrantly exceed the speed limit.

The outliers would be only individuals worthy of analysis. So in this case the majority of the data being captured would be useless or noise (Chen, Mao, & Liu, 2014; Chui, Löffler, & Roberts, 2010).

Advanced Scientific Research

Another area responsible for the explosive growth of data is the conduct of advanced scientific research. As computing power increases and the capability to develop powerful statistical and other models evolve, scientific research can utilize larger data sets than ever before. Some fields have experienced a renaissance of sorts with the advances in big data. An area of science growing rapidly along with big data is astronomy. In 1998, the Sloan Digital Sky Survey (SDSS) began as a means to record the visible area of space (visible by technological means). Over a ten year period SDSS stored 25 terabytes of data. As the optical capabilities of the SDSS telescopes improve there is anticipation that in the near future researchers may start capturing 20 terabytes of data per night (Aihara, et al., 2011). Another profound producer of big data is the Atlas research project being conducted by the Large Hadron Collider project of the European Council for Nuclear Research (CERN). On a monthly basis, the Atlas research effort produces approximately two petabytes of information from its testing activities (Rooney, 2011). Another discipline experiencing high data growth is computational biology. The US National Biotechnology Innovation Center maintains a database called Genbank, storing

DNA and RNA sequences for over 250,000 unique life forms.   By late 2009, Genbank stored roughly 450 billion bytes of genetic information for those life forms (Benson, et al., 2012; Chen, Mao, & Liu, 2014).

The Value of Big Data

After conducting in-depth research, McKinsey & Company noted how big data has already created value in the following domains of economic activity: Health care, public management, retail businesses, global manufacturing, and personal location data. Based upon research in these five core areas of the global economy, McKinsey pointed out that big data can enhance productivity and competitiveness of businesses and the public sector, enable economic value in certain areas, and create enormous gains for consumers (Chen, Mao, & Liu, 2014; Manyika, et al., 2011).   The five domains listed above reflected 40 percent of the entire world's GDP in 2010.   The McKinsey study made some well-founded statements on the economic worth big data could provide.   The following sections will address the key points and issues in three of the top areas, US health care, retail, and public management.

US Health Care

If big data could be creatively used to enhance efficiency and quality, the value of savings in the US health care sector could surpass US$300 billion, thereby reducing the cost of health care by over 8% (Manyika, et al., 2011).

Big data strategies would bring much of this savings to bear through implementation in the following areas: clinical operations, payment/pricing, research and development, new business models, and public health (Manyika, et al., 2011).

Clinical Operations. Clinical operations include the systems and actions undertaken by providers to deliver care. McKinsey estimates that if big data strategies are developed to address particular business challenges in this area that an overall decrease of US$165 billion in costs could occur per year. Areas for prime utilization of big data are clinical decision support systems, the secured sharing of medical data, remote patient monitoring, and using advanced analytics to create custom care plans (Manyika, et al., 2011).

Payment and Pricing. Health care providers submit millions of claims on a yearly basis. There are optimizations which can be deployed to improve efficiencies and with such a large volume of transactions. In addition, there can be considerable costs savings with the optimal utilization of baseline data. Big data can help automate processes by delivering machine learning routines to identify fraud and errors. Big data can also be utilized in post-care settings to identify successful patient outcomes or identify treatment plans with less than optimal results. McKinsey estimates that US$50 billion could be saved through new processes in this area alone (Manyika, et al., 2011).

Research and Development. Research and development is a significant component of the pharmaceutical and medical products (PMP) sector of health care. The usage of big data in the scientific discovery process and subsequent engineering efforts stands to create up to US$100 billion in value. Advanced statistical processes will allow for improvement of not only the speed of clinical research but also the quality of findings (Manyika, et al., 2011).

New Business Models. Big data can also lead to the creation of entirely new business models within health care. Vast data sets from clinical to claims data can be analyzed and combined where appropriate to help in the diagnosis of disease, improve customer service, and post-discharge care. Big data can also be used to create new forums or communities for patients to learn about their conditions and anonymously share experiences (Manyika, et al., 2011).

Public Health. One notable use of big data that is already underway in the health care sector is the application of data sets in the management of public health events. Big data can not only utilize a widely dispersed set of patient and clinical data but can also be useful in detecting trends that would be otherwise unde-tectable. In 2009 during the peak of the H1N1 flu pandemic, Google supported a project analyzing publicly available data to monitor any postings or comments related to flu or related symp-toms. The decision was made to focus on Twitter feeds (also known as Tweets) due to their near real-time nature. The Google project revealed patterns in messages that were closely related to upcoming concentrations of flu outbreaks. Ultimately Google was able to create models forecasting the spread of the flu (Ginsberg, et al., 2008; Manyika, et al., 2011).

Retail

Retailers that efficiently use big data could improve their profits by more than 60% (Manyika, et al., 2011). Marketing and mer-chandising are critical areas where big data can provide tremen-dous value to retailers.

Marketing. Retailers stand to benefit significantly in the area of marketing through the use of big data. Techniques such as sen-timent analysis, location-based marketing, cross-selling, and in-store behavior analysis can all help improve profitability consider-ably (Manyika, et al., 2011). Amazon reported that its recommendation engine ("customers like you also bought this") was responsible for 30 percent of its sales in 2012 (Matthews, 2012). Big data supports the just-in-time pairing of purchases with highly likely co-selling add-ons. In the realm of location-based marketing, the firm PlaceCast sponsored research which shows that nearly 50 percent of customers will respond favorably to an ad for a retailer in their immediate location if delivered via mobile phone (ABI Research, 2010). Retailers are also finding great value in analyzing the store navigation patterns of customers and then their final purchases. Such deep data analysis can help improve product placement, as well as planning for promotions or co-selling opportunities. The area of sentiment analysis is a potentially ripe area of big data utilization. In the past retailers relied on focus groups and formal surveys to receive feedback on new ideas or products. Twitter and Facebook provide a broad base of easy to access customer impressions. These platforms also offer the capability for retailers to interact with customers in a personal yet public manner (Manyika, et al., 2011).

Merchandising. Merchandising in the retail context refers to any factor that relates to products for sale within a store. This can involve pricing decisions, product placement on shelves, or even removing products from the floor. Big data can be utilized significantly in any merchandising strategy. Assortment optimization is the process of picking products to place on display based on demographics or other information gained from large data sets. McKinsey reported a case study of a drug store that undertook an analytics effort to find out the causes for the stagnation of certain products. The store ultimately reduced its overhead, increased placement of private-label brands, and drove a three-percent growth in earnings (Manyika, et al., 2011). Retailers have also begun to perform data mining on sales data and correlating those findings with product placement on the shelves to create strategies to boost sale rates. Similarly retailers with an online-only presence (or a primary online presence) utilize click-through analysis to determine the optimal page layout and design practices (Manyika, et al., 2011).

Public Management

Big data may additionally be used to enhance the efficacy of government activity. For instance, European nations could save over €100 billion according to research by McKinsey (this total does not include the effect of fraud recapture, reducing errors, and improved taxation efficiencies) (Manyika, et al., 2011). Governments can exploit the value of big data in many ways, but the following areas will provide the most immediate return on investment for innovation: Improving transparency and decision-making while reducing costs, creating personalized citizen experiences, reducing tax and social security fraud, and promoting the safety and health of citizens and the state (Manyika, et al., 2011).

Improving Transparency and Decision-Making While Reducing Costs. Governments are in a unique position since they hold vast repositories of data. One frequent chore of citizens is the need to fill out forms such as those related to paying taxes on an annual basis. Systems that can generate pre-filled forms for taxpayers not only save time for the citizens but reduce errors related to data processing. The Swedish Tax Agency instituted a process of sending residents pre-filled tax forms. It also allows citizens the ability to modify those tax forms via short message service (SMS) or the Internet. The Netherlands tax agency also instituted a similar effort where they cross reference employer provided information and bank account details when pre-filling tax forms for their citizens (Manyika, et al., 2011).

Governments around the world are also adopting a trend of making data publicly available. Data.gov in the US, the Aporta portal in Spain, and Data.gov.uk in the United Kingdom are all consolidated repositories where citizens can examine and download several hundred data sets from many aspects of their government's activities (Manyika, et al., 2011). One notable service exhibiting this practice is the ITDashboard.gov website in the US. This website makes available the current financial and project status of IT programs across all of the US Cabinet agencies.

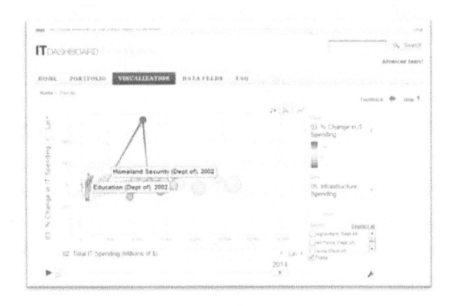

Figure 4: The US Federal Government IT Dashboard

Another aspect of increased transparency is that citizens can now see how officials spend the public's money.   Big data can allow the identification of fraudulent or suspicious travel. In addition, it can drive value-based decisions on the benefits of travel as well as create standards by which to decide for or against cases of unneeded travel (Manyika, et al., 2011).

Personalization of Government-Citizen Interaction.   Big data can also allow governments more refined capabilities at offering highly personalized benefits and services.   Personalization is particularly useful in response to crises or sudden economic events. Benefits selection can now be conducted rapidly with predefined algorithms to find and detect citizens who meet certain criteria for need-based benefits. This type of segmentation is widely used in the commercial sector, and it has a strong use case in the public sector (Manyika, et al., 2011).

Advanced technologies related to big data can also be leveraged to analyze citizen sentiment in response to proposed legislation or gather feedback on changes in program administration. Citizen inquiries to call centers could also be analyzed to determine the need for services such as a new park or a public health facility.

A powerful example of the use of big data in a personalized capacity comes from Germany. The Bundesagentur für Arbeit / German Federal Labor Agency (also referred to as the BA) mined its data stores to uncover key trends and details. The BA focused on data related to unemployment, interventions undertaken by the agency, and the length of time required for citizens to return to work. The goal of the BA was to create classifications of workers and then develop specific programs to help return those individuals to work. Over a period of three years, the BA applied its segmentation strategy, to reduce its spending level by €10 Billion (US$14.9 billion). The BA also created an increased level of customer satisfaction (WCC, 2014; Manyika, et al., 2011).

Fraud Detection and Analysis. Fraud is a major concern for

any government entity. As stewards of public funds, governments must aggressively seek out, halt, and punish those who cheat the government. Big data provides a powerful new capability to not only mine large data sets for suspicious patterns but conduct analysis across data sets to unlock relationships that were not recognized before and uncover fraudulent behavior. Governments at many levels utilize data sets to gain a 360-degree perspective to understand unexplained wealth or excessive filing of claims (Manyika, et al., 2011).

The Centers for Medicare and Medicaid Services, the primary US government agency providing health care coverage to the elderly and indigent, is utilizing big data analytics to unearth claims that might be fraudulent even before a payment is made. Predictive analytic routines scour claims in the preprocessing phase for records with specific qualities. This supervised machine learning system is known as the Fraud Prevention System and operates in real time. The system has identified and prevented what would have been US$115 million in fraudulent payments. That dollar amount corresponds to a savings of US$3 for every US$1 spent on the programs' initial funding (Centers for Medicare & Medicaid Services, 2013; Manyika, et al., 2011).

Public Safety. For the efficient execution of law enforcement, it is vital for police departments to understand current as well as historical factors related to crime. The City of Las Vegas (Nevada)

Police Department developed a set of advanced algorithms against a vast historical database and other data sources, such as weather and event data, to predict areas and times where crime is likely to occur. The police department uses this data to adjust manpower levels as needed to conduct effective patrols (Manyika, et al., 2011; Shlayan & Kachroo, 2012).

Another significant big data usage by government is the travel monitoring responsibility of the US Department of Homeland Security (DHS). The DHS monitors the travel of more than two million passengers who fly daily into or within the US. The DHS also monitors more than one million people who cross the US borders by land or enter at a seaport. The DHS must analyze and assess an individual's "threat" level in seconds or else the flow of commerce can come to a complete halt. Such data analysis goes beyond just finding threats because the overwhelming majority of individuals pose no threat at all (Podesta, Pritzker, Moniz, Holdren, & Zients, 2014).

Governments must not only protect the physical safety of their citizens but also protect data related to those citizens. Given the vast amounts of sensitive information stored by governments, there is little doubt that criminals are interested in exploiting those records for nefarious purposes. Big data does present new challenges and issues for governments, but the potential benefits which can be gained are well worth the work to address those points.　Governments are poised to improve the overall health of communities, make public places safer, help build a vibrant economy, and offer timely and tailored public services (Manyika, et al., 2011).

Big Data as a Career Field

Given current state of opportunity within the field of big data and advanced analytics there is a high demand for individuals with skills related to this field.　Marketplace demands have resulted in the creation of a new job title, Data Scientist.　The Harvard Business Review declared Data Scientist to be the "sexiest" job for the 21st Century (Davenport & Patil, 2012).　Data Scientists are individuals who can solve advanced data analysis problems through the use of expert skills from the realms of computer science, statistics, and mathematics.　A keen understanding of business goals and strategy also helps refine the focus of a Data Scientist making their work more efficient, but a business-oriented skill-set is very rare.　Therefore, Data Science must typically be practiced as part of team effort because it is very unlikely that one individual will possess expert skills across all of these domains.　There is a significant global shortage of Data Scientists and individuals with other critical skills needed to support big data efforts (Davenport & Patil, 2012).　Some of these other skills include business-oriented data analytics skills and technical skills related to hardware and database administration.

Analysis conducted by McKinsey estimated that in 2008 only 150,000 people in the US were Data Scientists. Adjusting to the present, taking into account new training efforts, and counting recent graduates the pool increases to 300,000 skilled individuals. This total however is insufficient to reach an expected demand of 440,000 to 490,000 Data Scientist positions by 2018 (Manyika, et al., 2011). In some respects, individuals with business-oriented data analytics skills are even more important as the growth of data continues. Individuals in this category do not need to have deep statistical or mathematical training, but simply need to understand how to conduct quantitative analysis to help drive business decisions. McKinsey identified a potential need for 4 million business-savvy data analysts and managers by 2018. The forecast for staffing these positions is even direr. The estimated pool of qualified individuals in the US is expected to be only 2.5 million in 2018 (Manyika, et al., 2011). Clearly efforts must be made to train individuals on how to use analytics tools and software vendors must develop tools that are easier for individuals to use.

3

Methodology

This study was designed to evaluate perceptions held by information technology (IT) professionals in regards to big data. The study focused on an assessment of IT professionals and their self-assigned understanding of big data in relation to their perceptions of the maturity, value, hype, and future trends of big data. The study also looked at big data understanding in conjunction with IT professionals occupying a managerial role. The framework for the study was a survey instrument administered on-line.

Sample Design

The theoretical study population was all IT professionals regardless of their particular job role. The actual study population was IT professionals in the United States. Using data provided by United States Bureau of Labor Statistics, the estimated number of IT professionals in the United States is slightly less than 4 million.

Job title	May 2010 employment	January 2015 *
Computer support specialists	607,100	661,739
Computer systems analyst	544,400	604,284
Software developers, applications	520,800	593,712
Software developers, systems software	392,300	455,068
Computer programmers	363,100	384,886
Network & computer system admins	347,300	395,922
Computer & information systems managers	307,900	335,611
Information Security Analysts, Web Developers, and Computer Network Architects	302,300	335,553
Database administrators	110,800	127,974
Total	**3,496,000**	**3,894,749**

* Estimate based on annual percent growth using
BLS forecasts to 2020

Table 1: IT Professionals in the United States (adapted from US Bureau of Labor Statistics)

For global applicability, it was assumed that in regards to a series of questions related to a particular technology family (in this case big data), that US IT professionals would hold no particularly different attitudes or preconceptions about big data than IT professionals in other parts of the world.

Survey respondents participated in the survey via a custom response form that was developed on Google Forms. Study participants received an invitation to participate in the survey via Twitter alerts and the use of LinkedIn's email tool.

Research Hypotheses

The five hypotheses guiding this research effort are listed below (in both null and alternate forms):

Hypothesis HO1 (null): An IT professional's understanding of the principles of big data and related technologies is independent of his / her responsibilities in a managerial capacity.

Hypothesis HA1 (alternate): An IT professional's understanding of the principles of big data and related technologies is dependent on his / her responsibilities in a managerial capacity.

Hypothesis HO2 (null): An IT professional's perception of the value of big data solutions is independent of his / her understanding of big data solutions.

Hypothesis HA2 (alternate): An IT professional's perception of the value of big data solutions is dependent on his / her understanding of big data solutions.

Hypothesis HO3 (null): An IT professional's expectation of beneficial future development in the area of big data technologies is independent of his / her understanding of big data solutions.

Hypothesis HA3 (alternate): An IT professional's expectation of beneficial future development in the area of big data technologies is dependent on his / her understanding of big data solutions.

Hypothesis HO4 (null): An IT professional's perception of hype in regards to the market recognition of big data technologies is independent of his / her understanding of big data solutions.

Hypothesis HA4 (alternate): An IT professional's perception of hype in regards to the market recognition of big data technologies is dependent on his / her understanding of big data solutions.

Hypothesis HO5 (null): An IT professional's perception of the maturity of big data and related technologies is independent of his / her understanding of big data solutions.

Hypothesis HA5 (alternate): An IT professional's perception of the maturity of big data and related technologies is dependent on his / her understanding of big data solutions.

Instrument

An on-line questionnaire was used for data collection. The questionnaire is included in its entirety in Appendix A.

<u>Survey Design</u>

Part one of the survey was used to gather key demographics on the respondent. Questions were asked to determine the principal IT responsibility held by the respondent. Questions were also asked to establish a baseline regarding the respondent's industry of employment, length of time with their employer, and length of time as an IT professional. Respondents were also asked if they work in a managerial role.

Part two of the survey was used to gain insight into the respondent's perception of big data as it related to their awareness of the maturity, value, hype, future trends, and understanding of big data solutions. This section consisted entirely of five-point Likert scale questions so as to pinpoint precise results from the survey audience.

Part three of the survey was used to gain insight into the respondent's interaction or observation of the deployment (or non-deployment) of big data solutions in their organization. Questions also measured the overall sense of importance of big data in their organization and who is the visionary for big data within their organization.

The entire survey consisted of twenty questions and contained no open-ended or narrative style questions. The expectation was that the survey could be completed in less than five minutes in virtually every administration.

Validity and Reliability

The survey instrument's validity was evaluated using pre-test assessments. The researcher examined similar IT-oriented survey models to determine if the technical orientation of the questions was appropriate. Since the study was not being administered to determine causality of action there was no reason to evaluate internal validity (Cooper & Schindler, 2010).

The survey instrument was however evaluated for reliability, to determine its durability of repeated results. The Cronbach Alpha was measured using the open source statistical software program PSPP and returned at a high co-efficiency of internal consistency at 0.96 which indicates strong reliability for the scaled section of the survey tool.

Variables

The scaled section of the survey consisted of six main variables to enable the evaluation of the hypotheses.

The variables are as follows: Managerial position, maturity, value, hype, future trends, and understanding of big data solutions.

Managerial position was evaluated using a simple 'yes/no' question to determine if the respondent occupies a supervisor role. This variable was assessed by question 5.

Maturity was the respondent's perception of big data as being a solution or set of technologies that are sufficiently developed to be used in a production capacity and are capable of generating value. This variable was assessed by question 6.

Value was the respondent's perception of big data solutions being worth time, effort, and resources required for deployment. This variable was assessed by question 7

Hype was the respondent's perception of the industry and other IT professionals overstating the usefulness, value, or ease of deployment of big data solutions. This variable was assessed by question 8.

Future trends was the respondent's perception of near-term future for advances in big data solutions and technologies. This variable was assessed by question 9.

Understanding was the respondent's perception of his or her

knowledge of the scope and individual components of big data solutions. This variable was assessed by question 10.

Data Collection

The collection of data, via an on-line survey tool, occurred over a one week period from August 5 to August 12, 2014. The survey was available twenty-four hours a day for the respondents.

To address any concerns about their responses being used in a manner that could directly affect their employment, all respondents were advised that results were confidential. They were also informed that the Google Forms survey tool stored no personally identifiable information along with their responses. Survey results were uniquely identified only by a data-time stamp in the co-located data collection spreadsheet.

Data Analysis

Each of the five hypotheses was tested using a One-Way Analysis of Variance test in the open source software PSPP with a significance level of 0.05.

Additionally cross-tabulations were prepared to examine the detail of responses across the Likert scale range when compared to the dependent variable.

Summary

This chapter discussed the methods used to create, administer and evaluate a survey to determine the perceptions held by IT professionals and the positions they occupy in relation to their perceptions of the maturity, value, hype, future trends, and understanding of big data solutions in their organizations or in the organizations that they support in a professional role. The survey was conducted using an online response form and results were analyzed using the One-Way Analysis of Variance test and detailed cross-tabulations for each hypothesis.

The next chapter will provide the results of the study, evaluation of each hypothesis, and discussion of each question administered on the questionnaire.

4

Data Collection and Analysis

This chapter presents the findings resulting from the study. This study was designed to evaluate perceptions held by information technology (IT) professionals in regards to big data. The study focused on an assessment of IT professionals and their self-assigned understanding of big data in relation to their perceptions of the maturity, value, hype, and future trends of big data. The study also looked at big data understanding in conjunction with occupying a managerial role. The study should prove helpful in determining linkages between training and awareness of big data and the ability of an organization to advance big data initiatives.

This chapter will evaluate each hypothesis and provide a discussion of the answers to each question on the questionnaire.

Results

There were 76 responses to the survey which represents an outstanding response rate for a survey administered solely by non-direct contact between the researcher and respondents. The number of responses exceeded a pre-study goal of 68 responses. With the overall population of IT professionals in the United States being an estimated 4 million this response rate allows a confidence interval of 90% to be established with a 9.5% +/- margin of error.

There was a relatively rapid initial response to the survey over the first two days with a few residual responses over the remaining period the survey was open.

There appear to be no indications of extreme views that might result from a non-response bias. In addition, it was assumed that the results accurately reflect the population since there was a good distribution of respondents with varying degrees of experience, fields of employment, and work role in the IT field.

Test of Hypothesis H1

Hypothesis H1 stated (null): An IT professional's understanding of the principles of big data and related technologies is independent of his / her responsibilities in a managerial capacity. This hypothesis was evaluated by comparing responses to question 5 and question 6 on the survey. Question 5 was "Do you occupy a role where you manage other IT staff?" Question 6 was "How would you categorize your understanding of big data?"

Based upon survey responses the respondents were divided into two groups, those who reported that they held a managerial role and those who said they did not. The One-Way Analysis of Variance of these groups had a p-value of .155, which is greater than the established significance level of .05. Based on these findings, the null is not rejected. The data produced insufficient evidence to conclude that being a manager has any impact on an individual's understanding of big data solutions.

	Sum of Squares	Df	Mean Square	F	Sig.
Between Groups	2.24	1	2.24	2.06	.155
Within Groups	80.12	74	1.08		
Total	82.36	75			

Table 2: One-Way Analysis of Variance – Hypothesis H1

		Big Data Understanding [1]					
		1	2	3	4	5	Total
Manager	Count	3.00	3.00	13.00	12.00	2.00	33.00
	Row %	9.09%	9.09%	39.39%	36.36%	6.06%	100.00%
	Column %	75.00%	33.33%	50.00%	46.15%	18.18%	43.42%
	Total %	3.95%	3.95%	17.11%	15.79%	2.63%	43.42%
Non-Manager	Count	1.00	6.00	13.00	14.00	9.00	43.00
	Row %	2.33%	13.95%	30.23%	32.56%	20.93%	100.00%
	Column %	25.00%	66.67%	50.00%	53.85%	81.82%	56.58%
	Total %	1.32%	7.89%	17.11%	18.42%	11.84%	56.58%
Total	Count	4.00	9.00	26.00	26.00	11.00	76.00
	Row %	5.26%	11.84%	34.21%	34.21%	14.47%	100.00%
	Column %	100.00%	100.00%	100.00%	100.00%	100.00%	100.00%
	Total %	5.26%	11.84%	34.21%	34.21%	14.47%	100.00%

[1] *Big Data Understanding*: 1-No Understanding, 2-Basic Understanding, 3-Familiarity, 4-Firm Understanding, 5-Understand Completely

Table 3: Managerial Status by Big Data Understanding - Raw Data

Test of Hypothesis H2

Hypothesis H2 stated (null): An IT professional's perception of the value of big data solutions is independent of his / her understanding of big data solutions. This hypothesis was evaluated by comparing responses to question 6 and question 8 on the survey. Question 6 was "How would you categorize your understanding of big data?" Question 8 was answered using a Likert scale with values starting with "Strongly Disagree" going to "Strongly Agree."

The statement was: "I feel that big data solutions are worth the investment of time, resources, and money."

Based upon survey responses the respondents were divided into five groups determined by their response to Question 6 assessing their understanding of big data solutions. The One-Way Analysis of Variance of these groups had a p-value of .205, which is greater than the established significance level of .05. Based on these findings, the null is not rejected. The data produced insufficient evidence to conclude that an individual's understanding of big data solutions impacts their perception of the value of big data solutions.

	Sum of Squares	Df	Mean Square	F	Sig.
Between Groups	3.78	4	.94	1.52	.205
Within Groups	44.01	71	.62		
Total	47.79	75			

Table 4: One-Way Analysis of Variance – Hypothesis H2

Big Data Under- standing [1]		Value of Big Data Solutions [2]					
		SD	D	N	A	SA	Total
1	Count	.00	.00	2.00	2.00	.00	4.00
	Row %	.00%	.00%	50.00%	50.00%	.00%	100.00%
	Column %	.00%	.00%	14.29%	4.76%	.00%	5.26%
	Total %	.00%	.00%	2.63%	2.63%	.00%	5.26%
2	Count	.00	.00	3.00	4.00	2.00	9.00
	Row %	.00%	.00%	33.33%	44.44%	22.22%	100.00%
	Column %	.00%	.00%	21.43%	9.52%	11.76%	11.84%
	Total %	.00%	.00%	3.95%	5.26%	2.63%	11.84%
3	Count	1.00	1.00	4.00	17.00	3.00	26.00
	Row %	3.85%	3.85%	15.38%	65.38%	11.54%	100.00%
	Column %	100.00%	50.00%	28.57%	40.48%	17.65%	34.21%
	Total %	1.32%	1.32%	5.26%	22.37%	3.95%	34.21%
4	Count	.00	1.00	4.00	14.00	7.00	26.00
	Row %	.00%	3.85%	15.38%	53.85%	26.92%	100.00%
	Column %	.00%	50.00%	28.57%	33.33%	41.18%	34.21%
	Total %	.00%	1.32%	5.26%	18.42%	9.21%	34.21%
5	Count	.00	.00	1.00	5.00	5.00	11.00
	Row %	.00%	.00%	9.09%	45.45%	45.45%	100.00%
	Column %	.00%	.00%	7.14%	11.90%	29.41%	14.47%
	Total %	.00%	.00%	1.32%	6.58%	6.58%	14.47%
Total	Count	1.00	2.00	14.00	42.00	17.00	76.00
	Row %	1.32%	2.63%	18.42%	55.26%	22.37%	100.00%
	Column %	100.00%	100.00%	100.00%	100.00%	100.00%	100.00%
	Total %	1.32%	2.63%	18.42%	55.26%	22.37%	100.00%

[1] *Big Data Understanding*: 1-No Understanding, 2-Basic Understanding, 3-Familiarity, 4-Firm Understanding, 5-Understand Completely

[2] *Value of Big Data Solutions*: SD-Strongly Disagree, D-Disagree, N-Neutral, A-Agree, SA-Strongly Agree

Table 5: Big Data Understanding by Assessment of Value - Raw Data

Test of Hypothesis H3

Hypothesis H3 stated (null): An IT professional's expectation of beneficial future development in the area of big data technologies is independent of his / her understanding of big data solutions. This hypothesis was evaluated by comparing responses to question 6 and question 10 on the survey. Question six is "How would you categorize your understanding of big data?" Question 10 was answered using a Likert scale with values starting with "Strongly Disagree" going to "Strongly Agree." The statement was: "I believe that there will be significant development and improvement in big data technologies over the next five years."

Based upon survey responses the respondents were divided into five groups determined by their response question number six assessing their understanding of big data solutions. The One-Way Analysis of Variance had a p-value of .001, which is less than the established significance level of .05. Based on these findings, the null is rejected. There is enough evidence to conclude that an individual's understanding of big data solutions impacts their perception of the value of big data solutions.

Since the null was rejected, the use of a Post-Hoc test following the One-Way Analysis of Variance is required to identify the groups between which there was the greatest difference.

The Post-Hoc Tukey Test was used to perform multiple comparisons of the means. Table 7 provides the results of the test. The p-value for big data understanding 1 vs. big data understanding 4 was .003, and the p-value for big data understanding 1 vs. big data understanding 5 was .003. Since these values are below the established significance level of .05, it can be concluded that the differences between these groups are significant.

	Sum of Squares	Df	Mean Square	F	Sig.
Between Groups	6.39	4	1.60	5.06	.001
Within Groups	22.40	71	.32		
Total	28.79	75			

Table 6: One-Way Analysis of Variance – Hypothesis H3

(I) Big Data Under-standing [1]	(J) Big Data Under-stand-ing [1]	Mean Dif-ference (I - J)	Std. Error	Sig.	Lower Bound	Upper Bound
1	2	-.94	.34	.050	-1.89	.00
	3	-.77	.30	.091	-1.61	.08
	4	-1.15	.30	.003	-2.00	-.31
	5	-1.23	.33	.003	-2.15	-.31
2	1	.94	.34	.050	.00	1.89
	3	.18	.22	.928	-.43	.78
	4	-.21	.22	.870	-.82	.40
	5	-.28	.25	.795	-.99	.42
3	1	.77	.30	.091	-.08	1.61
	2	-.18	.22	.928	-.78	.43
	4	-.38	.16	.110	-.82	.05
	5	-.46	.20	.168	-1.02	.11
4	1	1.15	.30	.003	.31	2.00
	2	.21	.22	.870	-.40	.82
	3	.38	.16	.110	-.05	.82
	5	-.07	.20	.996	-.64	.49
5	1	1.23	.33	.003	.31	2.15
	2	.28	.25	.795	-.42	.99
	3	.46	.20	.168	-.11	1.02
	4	.07	.20	.996	-.49	.64

[1] _Big Data Understanding_: 1-No Understand-ing, 2-Basic Understanding, 3-Familiarity, 4-Firm Understanding, 5-Understand Com-pletely

Table 7: Multiple Comparisons of Means / Tukey Test

		Future Growth of Big Data Solutions / Technology [2]					
Big Data Under-standing [1]		**SD**	**D**	**N**	**A**	**SA**	**Total**
1	Count	.00	.00	2.00	2.00	.00	4.00
	Row %	.00%	.00%	50.00%	50.00%	.00%	100.00%
	Column %	.00%	.00%	40.00%	6.25%	.00%	5.26%
	Total %	.00%	.00%	2.63%	2.63%	.00%	5.26%
2	Count	.00	.00	.00	5.00	4.00	9.00
	Row %	.00%	.00%	.00%	55.56%	44.44%	100.00%
	Column %	.00%	.00%	.00%	15.63%	10.26%	11.84%
	Total %	.00%	.00%	.00%	6.58%	5.26%	11.84%
3	Count	.00	.00	2.00	15.00	9.00	26.00
	Row %	.00%	.00%	7.69%	57.69%	34.62%	100.00%
	Column %	.00%	.00%	40.00%	46.88%	23.08%	34.21%
	Total %	.00%	.00%	2.63%	19.74%	11.84%	34.21%
4	Count	.00	.00	1.00	7.00	18.00	26.00
	Row %	.00%	.00%	3.85%	26.92%	69.23%	100.00%
	Column %	.00%	.00%	20.00%	21.88%	46.15%	34.21%
	Total %	.00%	.00%	1.32%	9.21%	23.68%	34.21%
5	Count	.00	.00	.00	3.00	8.00	11.00
	Row %	.00%	.00%	.00%	27.27%	72.73%	100.00%
	Column %	.00%	.00%	.00%	9.38%	20.51%	14.47%
	Total %	.00%	.00%	.00%	3.95%	10.53%	14.47%
Total	Count	.00	.00	5.00	32.00	39.00	76.00
	Row %	.00%	.00%	6.58%	42.11%	51.32%	100.00%
	Column %	.00%	.00%	100.00%	100.00%	100.00%	100.00%
	Total %	.00%	.00%	6.58%	42.11%	51.32%	100.00%

[1] _Big Data Understanding_: 1-No Understanding, 2-Basic Understanding, 3-Familiarity, 4-Firm Understanding, 5-Understand Completely

[2] _Future Growth of Big Data Solutions / Technology_: SD-Strongly Disagree, D-Disagree, N-Neutral, A-Agree, SA-Strongly Agree

Table 8: Big Data Understanding by Assessment of Big Data Future Growth - Raw Data

Test of Hypothesis H4

Hypothesis H4 stated (null): An IT professional's perception of hype in regards to the market recognition of big data technologies is independent of his / her understanding of big data solutions. This hypothesis was evaluated by comparing responses to question 6 and question 9 on the survey. Question six is "How would you categorize your understanding of big data?" Question 9 was answered using a Likert scale with values starting with "Strongly Disagree" going to "Strongly Agree." The statement was: "I believe that there is a significant amount of hype in the marketplace in relation to big data."

Based upon survey responses the respondents were divided into five groups determined by their response question number six assessing their understanding of big data solutions. The One-Way Analysis of Variance had a p-value of .017, which is less than the established significance level of .05. Based on these findings, the null is rejected.

Since the null was rejected, the use of a Post-Hoc test following the One-Way Analysis of Variance is required to identify the groups between which there was the greatest difference.

The Post-Hoc Tukey Test was used to perform multiple comparisons of the means. Table 6 provides the results of the test.

The p-value for big data understanding 3 vs. big data understanding 4 was .023. Since this value is below the established significance level of .05, it can be concluded that the differences between these groups are significant.

	Sum of Squares	Df	Mean Square	F	Sig.
Between Groups	6.68	4	1.67	3.25	.017
Within Groups	36.48	71	.51		
Total	43.16	75			

Table 9: One-Way Analysis of Variance – Hypothesis Four

(I) Big Data Under-standing [1]	(J) Big Data Under-stand-ing [1]	Mean Dif-ference (I - J)	Std. Error	Sig.	Lower Bound	Upper Bound
1	2	-.50	.43	.773	-1.71	.71
	3	-.35	.38	.896	-1.42	.73
	4	-.96	.38	.103	-2.04	.12
	5	-.68	.42	.484	-1.85	.49
2	1	.50	.43	.773	-.71	1.71
	3	.15	.28	.981	-.62	.93
	4	-.46	.28	.462	-1.24	.31
	5	-.18	.32	.980	-1.08	.72
3	1	.35	.38	.896	-.73	1.42
	2	-.15	.28	.981	-.93	.62
	4	-.62	.20	.023	-1.17	-.06
	5	-.34	.26	.691	-1.06	.39
4	1	.96	.38	.103	-.12	2.04
	2	.46	.28	.462	-.31	1.24
	3	.62	.20	.023	.06	1.17
	5	.28	.26	.814	-.44	1.00
5	1	.68	.42	.484	-.49	1.85
	2	.18	.32	.980	-.72	1.08
	3	.34	.26	.691	-.39	1.06
	4	-.28	.26	.814	-1.00	.44

[1] *Big Data Understanding: 1-No Understanding, 2-Basic Understanding, 3-Familiarity, 4-Firm Understanding, 5-Understand Completely*

Table 10: Multiple Comparisons of Means / Tukey Test

Big Data Under- standing [1]		SD	D	N	A	SA	Total
		Is There Significant Hype Related to Big Data [2]					
1	Count	.00	.00	2.00	2.00	.00	4.00
	Row %	.00%	.00%	50.00%	50.00%	.00%	100.00%
	Column %	.00%	.00%	16.67%	5.26%	.00%	5.26%
	Total %	.00%	.00%	2.63%	2.63%	.00%	5.26%
2	Count	.00	.00	1.00	7.00	1.00	9.00
	Row %	.00%	.00%	11.11%	77.78%	11.11%	100.00%
	Column %	.00%	.00%	8.33%	18.42%	4.17%	11.84%
	Total %	.00%	.00%	1.32%	9.21%	1.32%	11.84%
3	Count	.00	1.00	6.00	15.00	4.00	26.00
	Row %	.00%	3.85%	23.08%	57.69%	15.38%	100.00%
	Column %	.00%	50.00%	50.00%	39.47%	16.67%	34.21%
	Total %	.00%	1.32%	7.89%	19.74%	5.26%	34.21%
4	Count	.00	.00	3.00	8.00	15.00	26.00
	Row %	.00%	.00%	11.54%	30.77%	57.69%	100.00%
	Column %	.00%	.00%	25.00%	21.05%	62.50%	34.21%
	Total %	.00%	.00%	3.95%	10.53%	19.74%	34.21%
5	Count	.00	1.00	.00	6.00	4.00	11.00
	Row %	.00%	9.09%	.00%	54.55%	36.36%	100.00%
	Column %	.00%	50.00%	.00%	15.79%	16.67%	14.47%
	Total %	.00%	1.32%	.00%	7.89%	5.26%	14.47%
Total	Count	.00	2.00	12.00	38.00	24.00	76.00
	Row %	.00%	2.63%	15.79%	50.00%	31.58%	100.00%
	Column %	.00%	100.00%	100.00%	100.00%	100.00%	100.00%
	Total %	.00%	2.63%	15.79%	50.00%	31.58%	100.00%

[1] *Big Data Understanding*: 1-No Understanding, 2-Basic Understanding, 3-Familiarity, 4-Firm Understanding, 5-Understand Completely

[2] *Significant Hype related to Big Data*: SD-Strongly Disagree, D-Disagree, N-Neutral, A-Agree, SA-Strongly Agree

Table 11: Big Data Understanding by Hype related to Big Data - Raw Data

Test of Hypothesis H5

Hypothesis H5 stated (null): An IT professional's perception of the maturity of big data and related technologies is independent of his / her understanding of big data solutions. This hypothesis was evaluated by comparing responses to question 6 and question 7 on the survey. Question six is "How would you categorize your understanding of big data?" Question 7 was answered using a Likert scale with values starting with "Strongly Disagree" going to "Strongly Agree." The statement was: "I believe that big data is a mature information technology framework."

Based upon survey responses the respondents were divided into five groups determined by their response question number six assessing their understanding of big data solutions. The One-Way Analysis of Variance had a p-value of .251, which is greater than the established significance level of .05. Based on these findings, the null is not rejected. The data produced insufficient evidence to conclude that an individual's assessment of big data being a mature information technology framework is based on their level of big data understanding.

	Sum of Squares	Df	Mean Square	F	Sig.
Between Groups	4.36	4	1.09	1.37	.251
Within Groups	56.27	71	.79		
Total	60.63	75			

Table 12: One-Way Analysis of Variance – Hypothesis Five

Big Data Under- standing [1]		Maturity of Big Data [2]					
		SD	D	N	A	SA	Total
1	Count	.00	.00	3.00	1.00	.00	4.00
	Row %	.00%	.00%	75.00%	25.00%	.00%	100.00%
	Column %	.00%	.00%	11.11%	5.88%	.00%	5.26%
	Total %	.00%	.00%	3.95%	1.32%	.00%	5.26%
2	Count	.00	4.00	3.00	2.00	.00	9.00
	Row %	.00%	44.44%	33.33%	22.22%	.00%	100.00%
	Column %	.00%	14.81%	11.11%	11.76%	.00%	11.84%
	Total %	.00%	5.26%	3.95%	2.63%	.00%	11.84%
3	Count	1.00	14.00	7.00	4.00	.00	26.00
	Row %	3.85%	53.85%	26.92%	15.38%	.00%	100.00%
	Column %	25.00%	51.85%	25.93%	23.53%	.00%	34.21%
	Total %	1.32%	18.42%	9.21%	5.26%	.00%	34.21%
4	Count	1.00	5.00	12.00	8.00	.00	26.00
	Row %	3.85%	19.23%	46.15%	30.77%	.00%	100.00%
	Column %	25.00%	18.52%	44.44%	47.06%	.00%	34.21%
	Total %	1.32%	6.58%	15.79%	10.53%	.00%	34.21%
5	Count	2.00	4.00	2.00	2.00	1.00	11.00
	Row %	18.18%	36.36%	18.18%	18.18%	9.09%	100.00%
	Column %	50.00%	14.81%	7.41%	11.76%	100.00%	14.47%
	Total %	2.63%	5.26%	2.63%	2.63%	1.32%	14.47%
Total	Count	4.00	27.00	27.00	17.00	1.00	76.00
	Row %	5.26%	35.53%	35.53%	22.37%	1.32%	100.00%
	Column %	100.00%	100.00%	100.00%	100.00%	100.00%	100.00%
	Total %	5.26%	35.53%	35.53%	22.37%	1.32%	100.00%

[1] *Big Data Understanding*: 1-No Understanding, 2-Basic
   Understanding, 3-Familiarity, 4-Firm Understanding, 5-
   Understand Completely
[2] *Maturity of Big Data*: SD-Strongly Disagree, D-
   Disagree, N-Neutral, A-Agree, SA-Strongly Agree

Table 13: Big Data Understanding by Assessment of the Maturity of Big Data - Raw Data

Detailed Responses

The next section will provide a detailed analysis of the answers for each question.

Question 1: The first question established a demographic baseline for the study and inquired about the IT role in which the respondent worked: "Please classify the primary role you fill as an IT professional."

The largest group of responses (39%) was "Analytics" which naturally matches up with the domain where big data is typically placed within information technology. The second highest group of responses was that of "MIS/IT Management" (30%). Together these two groups constituted 69% of all respondents.

Since individuals self-selected for the survey it makes sense that based on the title of the survey that analytics professionals would feel more comfortable answering the questions. Future survey options could benefit from recruiting a more distributed pool of respondents to amplify or mute the significance of data gained from the study.

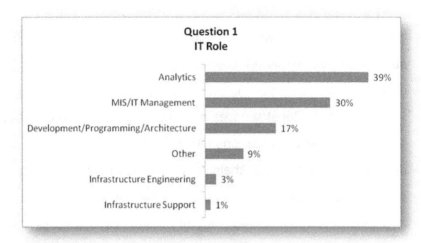

Figure 5: Question 1 – IT Role

IT Role	Count	Percentage
Analytics (Business Intelligence, Statistics, System Analysis)	30	39%
MIS/IT Management (CIO, VP, Director, Manager, Other)	23	30%
Development/Programming/Architecture (Desktop, Web, User Interface/Experience)	13	17%
Other	7	9%
Infrastructure Engineering (System/Network/Database Administration or Engineering, Security)	2	3%
Infrastructure Support (Help Desk, Installation, QA, Technical Writing, Training)	1	1%

Table 14: Question 1 – IT Role

Question 2: The second question gathered demographics on the industries in which the respondents were employed: "Please classify the primary industry in which you work."

The largest group of responses (58%) was "IT/Technology/Software/Computer related" this again is reasonable given the nature of the survey topic. The second highest group of responses was that of "Professional Services" (11%). A variety of professional services firms currently provide consultative services so that organizations can quickly identify and enable big data solutions relative to their needs and industry. The two largest groups of responses constituted 69% of all respondents.

There were respondents from all possible categories except for "Transportation and Construction."

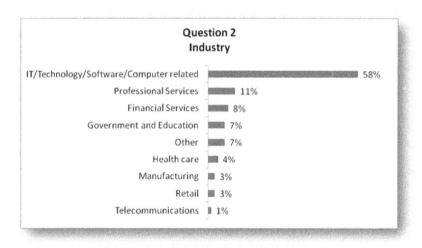

Figure 6: Question 2 – Industry of Employment

Industry	Count	Percentage
IT/Technology/Software/Computer related	44	58%
Professional Services	8	11%
Financial Services	6	8%
Other	5	7%
Government and Education	5	7%
Health care	3	4%

Table 15: Question 2 – Industry of Employment

Question 3: The third question measured the tenure of IT professionals at their current employer: "How many years have you been employed by your current organization?"

The largest group of responses (32%) was "Between 2 years and less than 5 years." The second highest group of responses was that of "Less than 1 year" (29%).   Together these two groups constituted 61% of all respondents.   The next highest group was "10 years or more" (18%).

The 18% finding for "10 years or more" is somewhat interesting and reflects the possibility that additional responses to the survey may be based on a significant pool of experience-driven encounters.

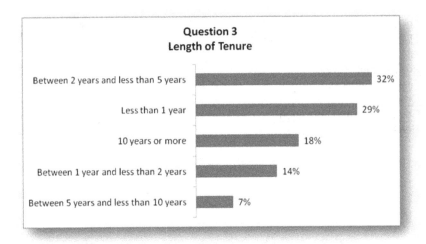

Figure 7: Question 3 – Tenure with current employer

Length of Tenure	Count	Percentage
Between 2 years and less than 5 years	24	32%
Less than 1 year	22	29%
10 years or more	14	18%
Between 1 year and less than 2 years	11	14%
Between 5 years and less than 10 years	5	7%

Table 16: Question 3 – Tenure with current employer

Question 4: The fourth question measured the overall tenure of IT professionals in the IT industry: "How many years have you been employed in the IT Industry?"

An overwhelming majority, 86%, reported that they had "10 years or more" work experience in IT. Adding the next highest group "Between 5 years and less than 10 years" (at 5%), 91% of all respondents reported greater than 5 years of experience.

This finding confirms that the pool of respondents has a great deal of experience and adds validity to the responses that relate to overall understanding of any IT solution, the value of an IT solution, and the maturity of any particular IT solution.   Lengthy tenures also reinforce the confidence that responses are particularly well thought-out since it is likely that the respondents have completed similar such surveys in the past.   However, it is possible that such a seasoned pool of respondents might be particularly well entrenched in their careers and may not have a strong awareness of more recent advances in the IT field. Future survey options could be administered with more focus on finding a more evenly distributed respondent pool with respect to career tenure.

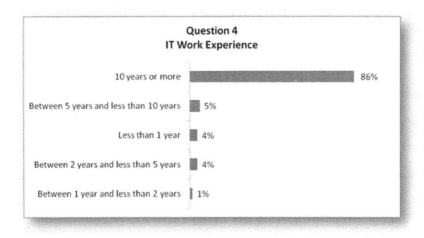

Figure 8: Question 4 – IT Work Experience

IT Work Experience	Count	Percentage
10 years or more	65	86%
Between 5 years and less than 10 years	4	5%
Between 2 years and less than 5 years	3	4%
Less than 1 year	3	4%
Between 1 year and less than 2 years	1	1%

Table 17: Question 4 – IT Work Experience

Question 5: The fifth question divided the respondent pool into two groups, manager and non-manager: "Do you occupy a role where you manage other IT staff?"

The division among respondents was fairly even with 57% reporting that they do manage other staff. This division allows for the ability to conduct cross-tabular analysis of any question against the manager/non-manager perspective. Hypothesis one utilized the responses to this question as the dependent variable.

For more precise cross-tabular analysis, a future study could evenly populate the manager/non-manager groups so that a genuine balance drives the corresponding analysis. For this study however the 57% to 43% ratio was more than adequate with only one hypothesis seeking to measure the impact of occupying a managerial position.

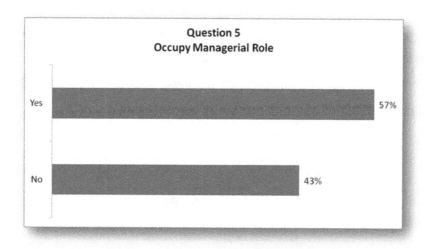

Figure 9: Question 5 – Do you manage other IT staff?

Occupy Managerial Role	Count	Percentage
Yes	43	57%
No	33	43%

Table 18: Question 5 – Do you manage other IT staff?

Question 6: The sixth question marked the beginning of the big data specific portion of the survey. This question measured the level of understanding of big data technologies by the respondent: "How would you categorize your understanding of big data?"

Two categories tied for the most responses "Firm Understanding" and "Familiarity" at 34%. Together these two groups constituted 68% of all respondents. Interestingly 5% of the respondents indicated they had "No Understanding" of big data technology.

The responses to this question were used in all of the statistical analysis operations in this study. Decisions related to future initiatives, training, and long-range planning are contingent on the understanding of any technology by current staff.

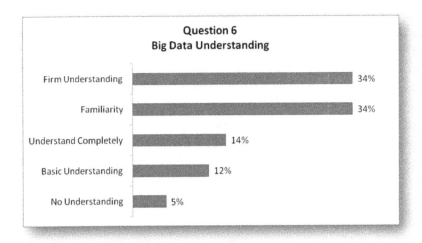

Figure 10: Question 6 – Big Data Understanding

Big Data Understanding	Count	Percentage
Familiarity	26	34%
Firm Understanding	26	34%
Understand Completely	11	14%
Basic Understanding	9	12%
No Understanding	4	5%

Table 19: Question 6 – Big Data Understanding

Question 7: The seventh question examined the degree to which the respondents regarded big data as being a mature IT framework or collection of tools: "I believe that big data is a mature information technology framework."

Two categories tied for the most respondents "Neutral" and "Disagree" at 36%. Together these two groups constituted 72% of all respondents.

This finding indicates, for the most part, that big data is still in a state of growth and evolution. Seventy-seven percent of respondents (when you include "Strongly Disagree") feel that big data still needs advancement before it is an assured technology like relational databases, for example. Future survey options could delve into the question of maturity more deeply to see if there is an issue with the tools used to build big data solutions or perhaps the tools used to create usable analytics and reporting from big data assets.

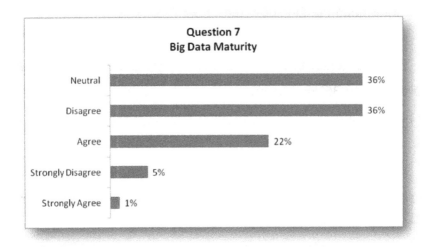

Figure 11: Question 7 – Assessment of the Maturity of Big Data

Assessment of the Maturity of Big Data	Count	Percentage
Disagree	27	36%
Neutral	27	36%
Agree	17	22%
Strongly Disagree	4	5%
Strongly Agree	1	1%

Table 20: Question 7 – Assessment of the Maturity of Big Data

Question 8: The eighth question examined the degree to which the respondents assessed the value of big data solutions and the extent to which pursuing them was worthwhile: "I feel that big data solutions are worth the investment of time, resources, and money."

The largest group of responses (55%) was "Agree." "Strongly

Agree" accounted for 22% of the responses. Together these two groups constituted 77% of all respondents.   The low rate of negative responses, "Disagree" at 3% and "Strongly Disagree" at 1% indicates an overwhelming majority of respondents see value in the pursuit of big data solutions.

Future survey options could attempt to target what particular aspects of big data solutions appear to offer the most value. This type of analysis would benefit enterprises significantly if a trend emerges around items like "uncovering deeply hidden trends" or "accessing widely disparate data sets in a homogenous manner."

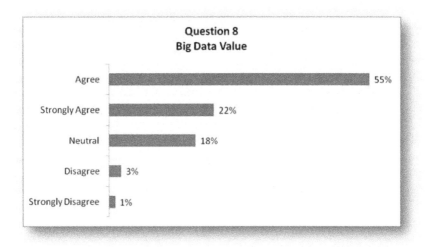

Figure 12: Question 8 – Assessment of the Value of Big Data

Assessment of the Value of Big Data	Count	Percentage
Agree	42	55%
Strongly Agree	17	22%
Neutral	14	18%
Disagree	2	3%
Strongly Disagree	1	1%

Table 21: Question 8 – Assessment of the Value of Big Data

Question 9: The ninth question attempted to gauge the degree to which the respondents felt that there was a lot of hype or unwarranted excitement surrounding big data solutions: "I believe that there is a significant amount of hype in the marketplace in relation to big data."

Fifty-one percent (51%) of the respondents agreed that there was a significant amount of hype. Even more strikingly, 32% stated that they strongly agreed meaning they felt that there was a significant amount of hype. These two categories combined represented 83% of all respondents, an overwhelming majority. This question also was the first of the Likert scale questions to not have a "Strongly Disagree" response. This indicates, along with the small pool of "Disagree" answers (3%), that a perception of hype exists in the IT community.

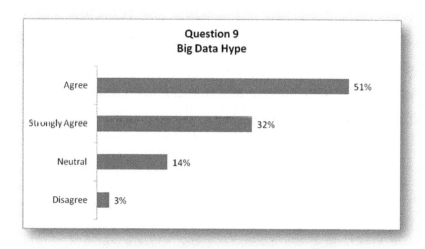

Figure 13: Question 9 – Assessment of Hype Surrounding Big Data

Assessment of Hype Surrounding Big Data	Count	Percentage
Agree	39	51%
Strongly Agree	24	32%
Neutral	11	14%
Disagree	2	3%
Strongly Disagree	0	0%

Table 22: Question 9 – Assessment of Hype Surrounding Big Data

Question 10: Question 10 measured the forward-looking perspective held by the respondents as it relates to big data: "I believe that there will be significant development and improvement in big data technologies over the next 5 years."

Fifty-one percent (51%) of the respondents strongly agreed that over the next five years there will be significant change and improvement in big data technologies. When coupled with the next highest response category, "Agree" at 42%, we see a very positive outlook for the future of big data (93%). In addition, this was the only Likert scale question to not have any "Disagree" or "Strongly Disagree" response.

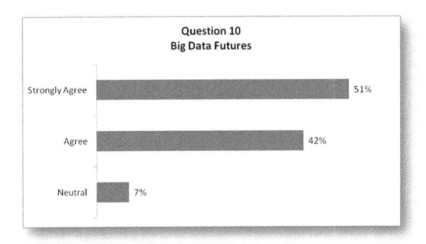

Figure 14: Question 10 – Assessment of Future Growth Related to Big Data

Assessment of Big Data Futures	Count	Percentage
Strongly Agree	39	51%
Agree	32	42%
Neutral	5	7%
Disagree	0	0%
Strongly Disagree	0	0%

Table 23: Question 10 – Assessment of Future Growth Related to Big Data

Question 11: Question eleven marked the start of the section covering big data topics from an organizational perspective. Specifically, question eleven was constructed to determine the most important issue related to big data: "From the list below, please select the one (1) item that you feel to be the biggest issue related to big data."

"Usable Analytics" received 34% of the responses. "Data Management" received 16%. Interestingly these two categories are most often aligned with the IT role associated with 39% of the respondents, analytics.

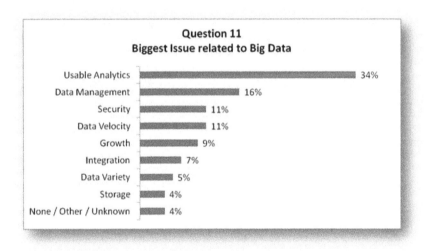

Figure 15: Question 11 – Biggest Issue Related to Big Data

Agreement	Count	Percentage
Usable Analytics	26	34%
Data Management	12	16%
Data Velocity	8	11%
Security	8	11%
Growth	7	9%
Integration	5	7%
Data Variety	4	5%
None / Other / Unknown	3	4%
Storage	3	4%

Table 24: Question 11 – Biggest Issue Related to Big Data

Question 12: Question 12 began a series of questions related to the context of big data within organizations. Specifically question 12 looked at the existence of a big data strategy: "Does the IT department in your organization (or that of your customer) currently have a defined strategy relating to big data and advanced analytics?"

Forty-five percent (45%) of the respondents stated that their IT departments did not have a defined strategy. Forty-one percent (41%) said yes, while 14% answered "Unknown." This data can indicate a few things. The first is that the IT department may have a big data strategy at some level or in some form, but they have not communicated it to the larger organization. However it can also mean that the IT department or the organization as whole does not have any strategy at all in place. These results indicate a strong need for education and identification of possible opportunities to deploy and use big data solutions.

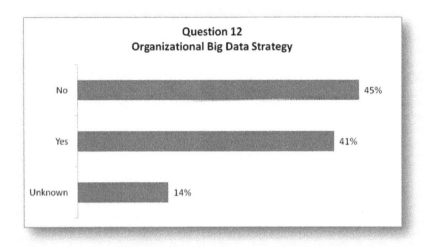

Figure 16: Question 12 – Organizational Big Data Strategy

Organizational Big Data Strategy	Count	Percentage
No	34	45%
Yes	31	41%
Unknown	11	14%

Table 25: Question 12 – Defined Big Data Strategy

Question 13: Question 13 looked at the manner in which big data or related technologies were being used within the respondent's organization. In particular the question examined what is a common use cases for big data – analysis of unstructured content: "Does your organization currently process or analyze unstructured data sources (Twitter, blogs, emails, employee evaluations, etc.) to gain new insight?"

Forty-seven percent (47%) of the respondents stated that such data sources were being analyzed in some shape or form. The question left open the possibility that technologies or frameworks other than big data could be used to analyze such sources of data. This indicates that additional research could be focused on this topic to see just how deeply big data has penetrated this area of analysis in organizations.

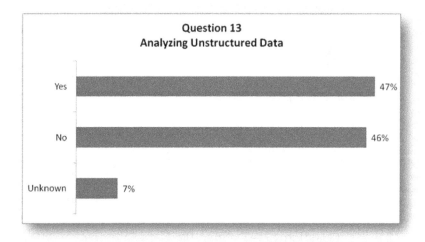

Figure 17: Question 13 – Analysis of Unstructured Data

Analyzing Unstructured Data	Count	Percentage
Yes	36	47%
No	35	46%
Unknown	5	7%

Table 26: Question 13 – Analysis of Unstructured Data

Question 14: Question 14 asked a very pointed question to assess the maturity or importance of big data within the respondent's organization: "Does your organization have employees with the job title 'Data Scientist'?"

A majority of respondents, 63%, indicated no employees in their organization had the job title 'Data Scientist'. While this finding alone does not positively mean that there are no pockets of big data related analytics, the presence of Data Scientists does indicate the organization has made a commitment to the usage of big data.

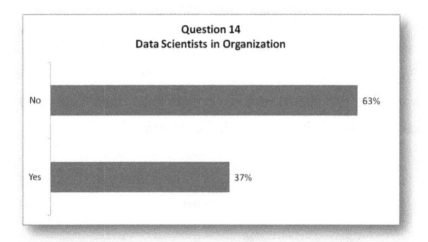

Figure 18: Question 14 – Employees with the Job Title 'Data Scientist'

Employees with the job title 'Data Scientist'	Count	Percentage
No	48	63%
Yes	28	37%

Table 27: Question 14 – Employees with the Job Title 'Data Scientist'

Question 15: Question 15 sought to measure the impact of big data on the respondent's organization and critical decision-making: "Please respond to the following statement: Big data has an impact on my organization. Many strategic decisions are based on data derived from big data and advanced analytics."

Forty-seven percent (47%) of the respondents agreed with the statement but a surprisingly large group, 17%, answered "Unknown." This response could reflect a few conditions. The first is that big data is either not being used or has not reached a level of practical usage in the organization. The second is that big data is being used in a blended way so that individuals are not even aware of it. Additional research on this topic could focus on the exact ways in which big data is being utilized.

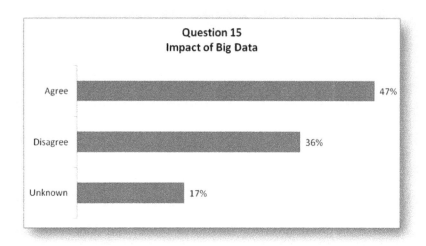

Figure 19: Question 15 – Impact of Big Data

Impact of Big Data	Count	Percentage
Agree	36	47%
Disagree	27	36%
Unknown	13	17%

Table 28: Question 15 – Impact of Big Data

Question 16: In order to gauge the sense of big data adoption and/or the lack thereof, question 16 evaluated activities within the respondent's organization: "Please categorize the level of big data activity for your organization (or that of your customer). Choose only one (1) value."

The largest group of responses, 36%, was "Deployed some Projects". The next three highest responses indicate that no concrete projects are in place, "Investigating" at 22%, "No Activity" at 16% and "Plan to initiate in 12 months" at 8%. The overall percentage that reflects some development or production activity is 49%. This percentage is in line with the rates associated with recognition of big data impacting the organization (47%) and analysis of unstructured data sets (47%).

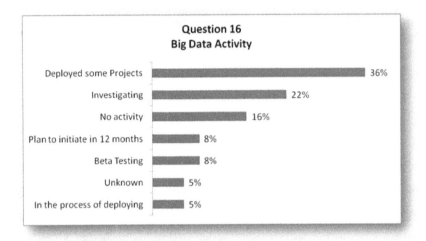

Figure 20: Question 16 – Big Data Activity

Big Data Activity	Count	Percentage
Deployed some Projects	27	36%
Investigating	17	22%
No activity	12	16%
Beta Testing	6	8%
Plan to initiate in 12 months	6	8%
In the process of deploying	4	5%
Unknown	4	5%

Table 29: Question 16 – Big Data Activity

Question 17: Question 17 sought to evaluate technical details related to the deployment of big data solutions in the respondent's organization: "What is the delivery mechanism for big data and advanced analytics in your organization?"

Not surprisingly given the previous responses indicating little to no activity related to big data, the top answer was "Unknown/None" at 36%. The next two responses reflect the divergent situation related to big data deployments. "Traditional data center / server based platform (on-premise)" reflected 32% of the responses while "Private and Public Cloud (Hybrid)" corresponded to 17%. This breakdown shows the shift in enterprise computing currently underway on a wider scale. Some organizations still feel they need to control IT assets in house while others recognize the agility and flexibility offered by cloud-based solutions. As indicated in the literature review there is much interest in maximizing time to value with big data initiatives by utilizing cloud-based resources. As a follow on to this study, updated research should be undertaken to see how much of the on-premise solutions have moved to the cloud.

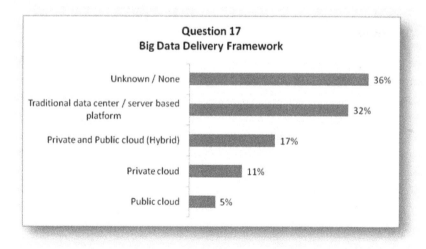

Figure 21: Question 17 – Big Data Delivery Framework

Big Data Delivery Framework	Count	Percentage
Unknown / None	27	36%
Traditional data center / server based platform	24	32%
Private and Public cloud (Hybrid)	13	17%
Private cloud	8	11%
Public cloud	4	5%

Table 30: Question 17 – Big Data Delivery Framework

Question 18: Question 18 was designed to gather the future-oriented perspective of big data in the respondent's organization: "Please categorize the importance/priority of big data and advanced analytics for your organization over the next 12 months."

Forty-one percent (41%) of the respondents said that big data was "Fairly Important." Along with the next highest response, "Top or Very High Priority" (20%), it can be assumed that most organizations believe that big data is quite important.

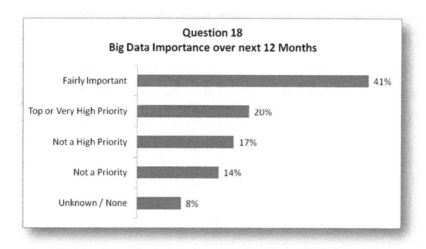

Figure 22: Question 18 – Big Data Importance over next 12 Months

Big Data Importance	Count	Percentage
Fairly Important	31	41%
Top or Very High Priority	15	20%
Not a High Priority	13	17%
Not a Priority	11	14%
Unknown / None	6	8%

Table 31: Question 18 – Big Data Importance over next 12 Months

Question 19: Question 19 was constructed to gather details on exactly how big data was being used in the respondent's organization: "From the list below, please select all relevant use cases related to big data currently undertaken by your organization."

Unlike other questions on the survey, this question allowed for multiple responses. This means that the percentages do not represent an absolute representation of applicability to the entire pool of respondents. It does however provide an excellent sense what seems to be important when it comes to big data solutions. "Gaining competitive advantage" was the most selected use case (43%). "Customer retention" (38%) and "Product development" (32%) were the next highest selected use cases.

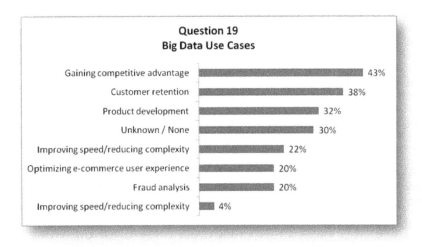

Figure 23: Question 19 – Big Data Use Cases

Big Data Use Cases (Multiple Answer)	Count	Percentage
Gaining competitive advantage	33	43%
Customer retention	29	38%
Product development	24	32%
Unknown / None	23	30%
Improving speed/reducing complexity	17	22%
Fraud analysis	15	20%
Optimizing e-commerce user experience	15	20%
Improving speed/reducing complexity	3	4%

Table 32: Question 19 – Big Data Use Cases

Question 20: The final question on the survey was developed to determine who in the respondent's organization is recognized as the leader or visionary of big data innovation: "From the list below, please select the leader in your organization who shows the most interest in big data and related activities"

There were many options available as answers for this question which led to relatively small percentages for each. The highest group of responses was "CEO/President" at 17%. There was a tie for the next highest group of responses. The "CIO" and "Other" each represented 16% of answers. No respondent reported the "CFO" as being the big data visionary.

Figure 24: Question 20 – Big Data Visionary

Big Data Visionary	Count	Percentage
CEO / President	13	17%
CIO	12	16%
Other	12	16%
None have expressed interest	9	12%
CMO/marketing leader	7	9%
Line-of-business director	7	9%
Chief Analytics Officer/Chief Data Scientist	6	8%
Sales leadership (VP/Director)	5	7%
COO	3	4%
Other C-Suite executive	2	3%
CFO	0	0%

Table 33: Question 20 – Big Data Visionary

Summary

This chapter discussed the findings resulting from the study. The chapter evaluated each hypothesis and provided a discussion of the answers to each question administered on the question-naire.

The next chapter will present conclusions from the study. It will also make recommendations for further study on big data and related topics.

5

Summary and Conclusions

This chapter addresses the findings and conclusions resulting from the study. This study investigated five research questions. 1) Is an IT professional's understanding of the principles of big data and related technologies influenced by the fact that they occupy a managerial role or not? 2) Is an IT professional's perception of the value of big data solutions influenced by their understanding of big data solutions or not? 3) Is an IT professional's expectation of beneficial future development in the area of big data technologies influenced by their understanding of big data solutions or not? 4) Is an IT professional's perception of hype in regards to the market recognition of big data technologies influenced by their understanding of big data solutions or not? And finally 5) Is an IT professional's perception of the maturity of big data and related technologies influenced by their understanding of big data solutions or not?

The study of big data related to its utilization in management contexts is a relatively new phenomenon since the creation data analysis related to big data has only been around for 10 – 15 years. As the technologies related to big data continue to evolve organically and from other existing technologies there will be specific methods to apply big data solutions to business problems. As such any research, which helps to guide decision-making in regards to identifying valid use cases and training for staff, will prove to be very beneficial.

Research Hypotheses

The following were the hypotheses for this study:

Hypothesis H1: An IT professional's understanding of the principles of big data and related technologies is independent of his / her responsibilities in a managerial capacity.

Hypothesis H2: An IT professional's perception of the value of big data solutions is independent of his / her understanding of big data solutions.

Hypothesis H3: An IT professional's expectation of beneficial future development in the area of big data technologies is independent of his / her understanding of big data solutions.

Hypothesis H4: An IT professional's perception of hype in regards to the market recognition of big data technologies is independent of his / her understanding of big data solutions.

Hypothesis H5: An IT professional's perception of the maturity of big data and related technologies is independent of his / her understanding of big data solutions.

Design

The population for the research study was theoretically all IT professionals in the United States. Respondents were recruited by Tweets on the Twitter platform and via LinkedIn emails. The survey consisted of three sections. The first section gathered basic demographic information about the respondent such as job role, industry, length of time with current firm, and length of time as an IT professional. The second section measured perceptions of big data understanding, solution maturity, solution value, marketplace hype, trends for future development, and the main way in which the respondent's organization is using big data. Section three consisted of questions related to the practical deployment of big data solutions within the respondent's organization.

Seventy-six respondents completed the survey. This outcome exceeded a pre-study goal of 68 and represented a very successful survey given the indirect recruitment methods via Twitter and LinkedIn. The data was downloaded from Google Forms and loaded into the open source software PSPP for statistical analysis.

Conclusions

The results from various statistical tests supported rejecting two of the five null hypotheses. Two nulls were rejected based on a One-Way Analysis of Variance. The first null rejected was for Hypothesis H3: An information technology professional's expectation of beneficial future development in the area of big data technologies is independent of his / her understanding of big data solutions. The second null rejected was for Hypothesis H4: An information technology professional's perception of hype in regards to the market recognition of big data technologies is independent of his / her understanding of big data solutions.

Hypothesis H3 scored at .001 on the One-Way Analysis of Variance test. This result was well below the threshold of .05 which indicates a strong connection between big data understanding and expectation of future development in big data technologies. Follow-on use of the Tukey test confirmed this finding and identified the greatest differences occurring between the lowest level of big data understanding (1) and two highest levels of big data understanding (4 and 5).

Hypothesis H4 scored at .017 on the One-Way Analysis of Variance test. This result placed it below the threshold of .05 which indicates a strong connection between big data understanding and recognition of hype related to big data technologies. Follow-on use of the Tukey test confirmed this finding and identified the greatest differences occurring between those responding with "Familiarity" and "Firm Understanding" as a characterization of their level of big data understanding.

Suggestions for Further Research

The findings of this study indicate that IT professionals are still becoming familiar with big data and related technologies. The study produced evidence that the more an individual knows about big data, the more they expect greater future developments and enhancements with the technology. With IT professionals expecting improvements in big data there is great optimism for the future of big data. The study also indicated a lot of future efforts are focused on big data.

Future research should focus more closely on the question of the maturity of big data solutions in an in-depth manner. Such a focused study could pinpoint if any issues exist with the tools used to build big data solutions or if there is an issue with the tools used to consume analytics derived from big data stores.

Another area of future inquiry could focus on the specific aspects of big data solutions that seem to generate the best return on investment. Enterprises could gain value by targeting efforts on big data solutions focusing on the key qualities identified such as items like "gaining competitive advantage", "customer retention", and "product development."

In terms of a technology-oriented study, updated research should be undertaken to see how many of the on-premise solutions identified by respondents moved to the cloud.

Finally, a research effort could be undertaken to examine the manner and methods by which big data acceptance and growth occurs in organizations. For instance, attention could be paid to the evolution of who fills the prime visionary role or what methods and techniques those individuals use to promote big data within their corresponding organizations.

Appendix A

References

ABI Research. (2010). Technology Barometer: Mobile. New York: ABI Research.

Agrawal, R., Imieliński, T., & Swami, A. (1993). Mining association rules between sets of items in large databases. ACM SIGMOD Record, 22(2), 207-216.

Aihara, H., Prieto, C. A., An, D., Anderson, S. F., Aubourg, É., Balbinot, E., & Gunn, J. E. (2011). The eighth data release of the Sloan Digital Sky Survey: first data from SDSS-III. The Astrophysical Journal Supplement Series, 193(2), 29.

Alpaydin, E. (2004). Introduction to machine learning. Cambridge, MA: MIT Press.

Bailey, K. D. (1994). Typologies and taxonomies: an introduction to classification techniques. Chicago: Sage.

Benson, D. A., Cavanaugh, M., Clark, K., Karsch-Mizrachi, I., Lipman, D. J., Ostell, J., & Sayers, E. W. (2012). GenBank. Nucleic Acids Research, 1-7.

Bryant, R., Katz, R. H., & Lazowska, E. D. (2008). Big-Data Computing: Creating Revolutionary Breakthroughs in Commerce, Science and Society. Washington, DC: Computing Research Association.

Bureau of Labor Statistics. (2014, January 8). Computer and Information Systems Managers. Retrieved from Bureau of Labor Statistics: http://www.bls.gov/ooh/management/computer-and-information-systems-managers.htm

Bureau of Labor Statistics. (2014, January 8). Computer and Information Technology Occupations. Retrieved from Bureau of Labor Statistics: http://www.bls.gov/ooh/computer-and-information-technology/home.htm

California State University - Long Beach. (n.d.). PPA 696 RE-SEARCH METHODS TESTS FOR SIGNIFICANCE. Retrieved from California State University - Long Beach: https://www.csulb.edu/~msaintg/ppa696/696stsig.htm

Cattell, R. (2011). Scalable SQL and NoSQL data stores. ACM SIGMOD Record, 39(4, 12-27.

Centers for Medicare & Medicaid Services. (2013). Fraud Prevention Toolkit. Retrieved from Centers for Medicare & Medicaid Services: http://go.cms.gov/1zzv0Yr

Chamberlin, D. D. (2012). Early history of SQL. Annals of the History of Computing, IEEE, 78-82.

Chang, F., Dean, J., Ghemawat, S., Hsieh, W. C., Wallach, D. A., Burrows, M. .., & Gruber, R. E. (2008). Bigtable: A distributed storage system for structured data. ACM Transactions on Computer Systems (TOCS), 26(2, 4.

Chen, H., Chiang, R. H., & Storey, V. C. (2012). Business Intelligence and Analytics: From Big Data to Big Impact. MIS quarterly, 36(4), 1165-1188.

Chen, M., Mao, S., & Liu, Y. (2014). Big Data: A Survey. Mobile Networks and Applications, 19(2, 171-209.

Cherniack, M., Balakrishnan, H., Balazinska, M., Carney, D., Cetintemel, U., Xing, Y., & Zdonik, S. B. (2003). Scalable Distributed Stream Processing. CIDR, 257-268.

Chowdhury, G. G. (2003). Natural language processing. Annual review of information science and technology, 37(1), 51-89.

Chui, M., Löffler, M., & Roberts, R. (2010). The internet of things. McKinsey Quarterly, 1-9.

Constine, J. (2012). How Big Is Facebook's Data? 2.5 Billion Pieces Of Content And 500+ Terabytes Ingested Every Day. Retrieved from TechCrunch: http://bit.ly/1nKWiHM

Cooper, D. R., & Schindler, P. S. (2010). Business research methods. New York: McGraw-Hill.

Cortes, C., & Vapnik, V. (1995). Support-vector networks. Machine learning, 20(3), 273-297.

Cukier, K. (2010). Data, data everywhere: A special report on managing information. Economist Newspaper.

Davenport, T. H., & Patil, D. J. (2012). Data Scientist. Harvard Business Review, 90, 70-76.

Dayhoff, J. E., & DeLeo, J. M. (2001). Artificial neural networks. Cancer, 91(S8), 1615-1635.

Dean, J., & Ghemawat, S. (2008). MapReduce: simplified data processing on large clusters. Communications of the ACM, 51(1), 107-113.

DeWitt, D., & Gray, J. (1992). Parallel database systems: the future of high performance database systems. Communications of the ACM, 35(6), , 85-98.

Dickey, D. A. (2012). Introduction to Predictive Modeling with Examples. Proceedings of 2012 SAS Global Forum (p. 337). Orlando, FL: SAS.

Edelstein, P. (2013). Emerging directions in analytics. Predictive analytics will play an indispensable role in healthcare transformation and reform. Health Management Technology, 34(1), 16-17.

Gantz, J., & Reinsel, D. (2011). Extracting value from chaos. IDC iview, 1-12.

Garlasu, D., Sandulescu, V., Halcu, I., Neculoiu, G., Grigoriu, O., Marinescu, M., & Marinescu, V. (2013). A big data implementation based on grid computing. Roedunet International Conference (RoEduNet) (pp. 1-4). Sinaia, Romania: Institute of Electrical and Electronics Engineers.

Gartner. (2013). IT Glossary - Big Data. Retrieved from Gartner: http://gtnr.it/1rP0ANn

Ghemawat, S., Gobioff, H., & Leung, S. T. (2003). The Google file system. ACM SIGOPS Operating Systems Review, 29-43.

Ginsberg, J., Mohebbi, M. H., Patel, R. S., Brammer, L., Smolinski, M. S., & Brilliant, L. (2008). Detecting influenza epidemics using search engine query data. Nature, 1012-1014.

Goda, K. (2009). Database Machine. In Springer, Encyclopedia of Database Systems (pp. 714-714). New York: Springer.

Goldschmidt, P. G. (2005). HIT and MIS: implications of health information technology and medical information systems. Communications of the ACM, 48(10, 68-74.

Hewitt, E. (2010). Cassandra: the definitive guide. Sebastopol, CA: O'Reilly Media, Inc.

Hilbert, M., & López, P. (2011). The world's technological capacity to store, communicate, and compute information. Science, 60-65.

Jagadish, H., Gehrke, J., Labrindis, A., Papakonstantinou, Y., Patel, J., Ramakrishnan, R., & Shaabi, C. (2014). Big Data and Its Technical Challenges. Communications Of The ACM, 57(7, 86-94.

KDnuggets. (2012). What analytics data mining, big data software you used in the past 12 months for a real project? Retrieved from KDnuggets: http://bit.ly/1s7epZB

Koomey, J. (2011). Growth in data center electricity use 2005 to 2010. Burlingame, CA: Analytical Press.

Lazar, N. (2012). The Big Picture: Big Data Hits the Big Time. Chance, 47-49.

Manyika, J., Chui, M. B., Bughin, J., Dobbs, R., Roxburgh, C., & Byers, A. H. (2011). Big data: The next frontier for innovation, competition, and productivity. New York: McKinsey Global Institute.

Marcus, S., Moy, M., & Coffman, T. (2007). Social network analysis. In D. Cook, & L. Holder, Mining Graph Data (pp. 443-467). Hoboken, NJ: Wiley.

Martin, B., Hanington, B., & Hanington, B. M. (2012). Universal methods of design: 100 ways to research complex problems, develop innovative ideas, and design effective solutions. Beverly, MA: Rockport Publishers.

Matthews, C. (2012). Future of Retail: How Companies Can Employ Big Data to Create a Better Shopping Experience. Retrieved from Time: http://ti.me/1lgaMe1

May, E. (2014). The power of analytics: harnessing big data to improve the quality of care. Healthcare Executive, 29(2), 18.

Mayer-Schönberger, V., & Cukier, K. (2013). Big data: A revolution that will transform how we live, work, and think. Boston: Houghton Mifflin Harcourt.

McLellan, C. (2013). Big data: An overview. Retrieved from ZDNet: http://www.zdnet.com/big-data-an-overview_p2-7000020785

National Institute of Standards and Technology. (2014). NIST Big Data Working Group. Retrieved from National Institute of Standards and Technology:: http://bigdatawg.nist.gov/home.php

Nature. (2008). Specials: Big Data. Retrieved from Nature: http://www.nature.com/news/specials/bigdata/index.html

Oza, N. C., & Russell, S. (2000). Online ensemble learning. AAAI-00 Proceedings, 1109.

Podesta, J., Pritzker, P., Moniz, E. J., Holdren, J., & Zients, J. (2014). Big data: seizing opportunities, preserving values. Retrieved from Executive Office of the President: http://1.usa.gov/1ky0reK

Rooney, B. (2011). You Want Big Data? Is CERN Big Enough For You? Retrieved from The Wall Street Journal - Tech Europe: http://on.wsj.com/UNWREC

Rosoff, M. (2012). Jeff Bezos: 'Gatekeepers Slow Innovation'. Retrieved from Business Insider: http://read.bi/1n748q8

Schoultz, M. (2014). Lego Innovation: An example of Crowdsourcing Design. Retrieved from Digital Spark Marketing: http://bit.ly/1rM1zhc

Schroeck, M., Shockley, R., Smart, J., Romero-Morales, D., & Tufano, P. (2012). Analytics: The real-world use of big data. Armonk, NY: IBM Institute for Business Value.

Shlayan, N., & Kachroo, P. (2012). Formal Language Modeling and Simulations of Incident Management. Intelligent Transportation Systems, 13(3), 1226-1234.

Shvachko, K., Kuang, H., Radia, S., & Chansler, R. (2010). The hadoop distributed file system. Mass Storage Systems and Technologies (MSST), 2010 IEEE 26th Symposium (pp. 1-10). Lake Tahoe, NV: IEEE.

Spohrer, J. (2013). Advancing Big Data for Public Good. Retrieved from Building a Smarter Planet: http://ibm.co/1rTkk5Z

Su, S., Chang, H., Copeland, G., Fisher, P., Lowenthal, E., & Schuster, S. (1980). Database machines and some issues on DBMS standards. Proceedings of the May 19-22, 1980, national computer conference (AFIPS '80) (pp. 191-208). New York: ACM.

Tankard, C. (2012). Big data security. Network security, 5-8.

United Nations. (2013). Big Data for Development: A primer. New York: United Nations.

Venter, J. C., Adams, M. D., Myers, E. W., Li, P. W., Mural, R. J., Sutton, G. G., & Beasley, E. (2001). The sequence of the human genome. Science, 1304-1351.

WCC. (2014). Case Study: Bundesagentur für Arbeit. Retrieved from WCC: http://bit.ly/1nVp3lRa

Appendix B

Survey

The following screenshot images represent the entire survey as viewed by the respondents:

Big Data Survey

Thank you for participating in this survey regarding Big Data. The data collected will be used as part of my Doctoral Dissertation.

All responses are completely anonymous and no personally identifiable information is collected. Results are uniquely recorded by time-stamp upon submission. No other values are captured.

Should you have any questions or concerns please contact me at @gmail.com

Sincerely,

Damon

* Required

Background Questions

1. Please classify the primary role you fill as an IT Professional: *

☐ Analytics (Business Intelligence, Statistics, System Analysis)

☐ Development/Programming/Architecture (Desktop, Web, User Interface/Experience)

☐ Infrastructure Engineering (System/Network/Database Administration or Engineering, Security)

☐ Infrastructure Support (Help Desk, Installation, QA, Technical Writing, Training)

☐ MIS/IT Management (CIO, VP, Director, Manager, Other)

☐ Other

2. Please classify the primary industry in which you work: *

- IT/Technology/Software/Computer related
- Manufacturing
- Health care
- Financial Services
- Telecommunications
- Professional Services
- Government and Education
- Transportation and Construction
- Energy
- Retail
- Other

3. How many years have you been employed by your current organization? *

- Less than 1 year
- Between 1 year and less than 2 years
- Between 2 years and less than 5 years
- Between 5 years and less than 10 years
- 10 years or more

4. How many years have you been employed in the IT Industry? *

- Less than 1 year
- Between 1 year and less than 2 years
- Between 2 years and less than 5 years
- Between 5 years and less than 10 years
- 10 years or more

5. Do you occupy a role where you manage other IT staff? *

- Yes
- No

Big Data Questions

6. How would you categorize your understanding of big data? *

No Understanding	Basic Understanding	Familiarity	Firm Understanding	Understand Completely
○	○	○	○	○

7. I believe that big data is a mature Information Technology framework *

Strongly Disagree	Disagree	Neutral	Agree	Strongly Agree
○	○	○	○	○

8. I feel that big data solutions are worth the investment of time, resources, and money *

Strongly Disagree	Disagree	Neutral	Agree	Strongly Agree
○	○	○	○	○

9. I believe that there is a significant amount of hype in the marketplace in relation to big data *

Strongly Disagree	Disagree	Neutral	Agree	Strongly Agree
○	○	○	○	○

10. I believe that there will be significant development and improvement in big data technologies over the next 5 years. *

Strongly Disagree	Disagree	Neutral	Agree	Strongly Agree
○	○	○	○	○

11. From the list below, please select the one (1) item that you feel to be the biggest issue related to big data: *

☐ Storage

☐ Data Velocity

☐ Growth

☐ Data Variety

☐ Usable Analytics

☐ Integration

☐ Data Management

☐ Security

☐ None / Other / Unknown

Big Data Questions - Organizational

Please answer these questions as they relate to your organization or that of your customer(s) if your role entails such interaction.

12. Does the IT department in your organization (or that of your customer) currently have a defined strategy relating to big data and advanced analytics? *

☐ Yes

☐ No

☐ Unknown

13. Does your organization currently process or analyze unstructured data sources (Twitter, blogs, emails, employee evaluations, etc.) to gain new insight? *

☐ Yes

☐ No

☐ Unknown

14. Does your organization have employees with the job title 'Data Scientist'? *

☐ Yes

☐ No

15. Please respond to the following statement: Big data has an impact on my organization. Many strategic decisions are based on data derived from big data and advanced analytics. *

☐ Agree

☐ Disagree

☐ Unknown

16. Please categorize the level of big data activity for your organization (or that of your customer). Choose only one (1) value. *

☐ No activity

☐ Investigating

☐ Plan to initiate in 12 months

☐ Beta Testing

☐ In the process of deploying

☐ Deployed some Projects

☐ Unknown

17. What is the delivery mechanism for big data and advanced analytics in your organization? *

☐ Private cloud

☐ Public cloud

☐ Private and Public cloud (Hybrid)

☐ Traditional data center / server based platform

☐ Unknown / None

Appendix B

18. Please categorize the importance/priority of big data and advanced analytics for your organization over the next 12 months *

☐ Top or Very High Priority

☐ Fairly Important

☐ Not a High Priority

☐ Not a Priority

☐ Unknown / None

19. From the list below, please select all relevant use cases related to big data currently undertaken by your organization *

You may choose as many as are relevant

☐ Fraud analysis

☐ Optimizing e-commerce user experience

☐ Gaining competitive advantage

☐ Product development

☐ Customer retention

☐ Improving speed/reducing complexity

☐ Unknown / None

Big Data and IT Professionals

20. From the list below, please select the leader in your organization who shows the most interest in big data and related activities *

☐ CEO / President

☐ COO

☐ CIO

☐ CFO

☐ Chief Analytics Officer/Chief Data Scientist

☐ CMO/marketing leader

☐ Other C-Suite executive

☐ Sales leadership (VP/Director)

☐ Line-of-business director

☐ None have expressed interest

☐ Other

Submit

Never submit passwords through Google Forms.

100%: You made it.